Introduction

C000090264

Introduction

This Pocket PAL explains in a concise, practical manner the full concept of Learning Style Analysis (LSA) and Teaching Style Analysis (TSA) assessment instruments, which have been created, refined and extended since the early 1990s and used in many different countries around the world.

The LSA pyramid below illustrates the 49 elements making up the six layers of the Learning Styles (LS) model, which allows a deep insight into students' true learning needs, revealing the interplay between biological and learned styl preferences in difficult learning situations.

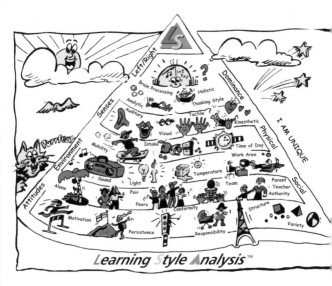

Learning Style Analysis™

For over three decades the term 'learning styles' has appeared in academic literature, often discredited, misinterpreted and dismissed as a concept that is either dangerous or doesn't really exist. It has almost been lost in educational theories which decree that bringing about change in classrooms and improving students' academic performance requires thorough research, is never easy and can certainly not be achieved by regular classroom teachers applying new teaching methods based on learning styles.

Well, thousands of teachers have done just that with great success, and the concept of learning styles is still around and gaining worldwide popularity. Particularly since the widespread use of the internet the LS concept has gained more followers than ever before. However, a word of caution is necessary here: not everything that is described as LS on approximately 250 websites is actually LS. Most tests and assessments are either very limiting, too simplistic, superficial and restrictive, or do not assess learning styles at all! Short tests cannot do justice to the complexity of biological and learned features that make up a person's full learning style profile. Only a comprehensive instrument such as the LSA can reveal full information about students' true learning needs in situations where they have to learn something new and/or difficult. This information gives teachers the guidelines for personalizing their teaching to draw out the learning potential every student has.

Throughout this Pocket PAL educators will find on the left-hand pages information about all aspects of LS and on the right-hand pages interpretations, explanations, applications and tips. By gaining a deeper understanding of style diversity in the classroom and using results from the LSA profiles, educators will be in a position to personalize their teaching strategies and adapt their curriculum delivery methods to accommodate their students' true learning needs. The result will be that fewer students are labelled as dyslexic, underachievers or as having 'special needs' or ADHD. These students *can* actually learn quite well – they just learn differently and often in a very unusual way, which teachers (and parents) find hard to comprehend.

False beliefs about learning

1. Students learn best when sitting upright at a desk.

2. Students learn best under bright light and damage their eyes when they read and work in low light.

3. Eating and drinking should not be permitted in classrooms.

Explanation

1. Research shows that many human beings function better in an informal environment. This is particularly true for children but most classrooms have wooden or plastic chairs and formal desks for students. When a person sits on such a chair, approximately 75 per cent of the total body weight is supported by only ten square centimetres of bone. The resulting stress on the tissues of the buttocks often causes fatigue, discomfort and the need for frequent postural change. Making students sit upright in their chairs does not necessarily help them learn better and often leads to agitated behaviour.

2. Research has shown that many students perform significantly better in low light environments, and bright light makes them restless, fidgety and hyperactive. Low light calms students, particularly holistic learners, and helps them relax and concentrate. Most underachievers need low light, and teachers are surprised by their improved behaviour, concentration and test results when they have been allowed to work in dim light.

    The younger children are, the less light they seem to need. They only need the amount of light for reading in which they feel comfortable. Need for light seems to increase every five years, which means adults need much more light than children do!

3. Many students concentrate better when they can eat, nibble, drink, chew, or bite while learning. Teachers are surprised to observe that students concentrate much better when allowed to nibble and/or have their own water bottle during learning sessions. If this is denied, students will still find something to chew on and teachers will never succeed in controlling that biological need.

Information

4. Students who do not sit still are not ready to learn.

5. Students learn difficult subjects best in the early morning when they are most alert.

6. The older students are, the easier it is for them to adapt to the teacher's style.

Explanation

4. Many students need mobility when they learn. One American study revealed that half of one school's grade seven students needed extensive mobility while learning. When they were allowed to move from one instructional area to another while learning new information, they achieved statistically better than when they had to remain seated. Most students who are actively involved are likely to learn more, pay closer attention and achieve higher test marks than when they just sit and listen!

5. Students who learn well in the morning are those we call 'early birds' – but what about the 'night owls' and 'afternoon learners' of the population? When a student is on task, the time preference is likely to be far more important than the subject or the amount of time spent on it! Research has shown that when students were allowed to learn at their preferred time of the day, their behaviour, motivation and maths scores improved. Taking tests at a preferred time means energy levels are at their highest and academic scores are significantly improved.

6. While older students require less teacher authority and less structure, they continue to learn differently from one another and have varying needs. Most need more independence as they grow older and develop stronger non-conformity features, often questioning authority. Therefore, it is appropriate to give them options for completing assignments and for required learning objectives. This gives them a chance to show their maturity and responsibility.

Information

LSA questionnaires

The gateway to LSA is through the appropriate questionnaire. These are freely available to use either as paper versions or online from the following websites:

www.creativelearningcentre.com/resources.asp
www.networkcontinuum.co.uk/LSA/index.html

Going through the statements of the questionnaire is in itself a very revealing process because students become aware of their style preferences by responding to detailed choices. For most students it is the first time in their lives that they have contemplated how they learn best when something is new and/or difficult.

The questionnaires are available for three age groups:
LSA-Junior (6-14 years of age);
LSA-Senior (14-18 years of age);
LSA-Adult (18+ years of age).

The questionnaires can then be processed online and detailed personal profiles can be purchased. These profiles will identify the student's preferred learning style and the accompanying guidelines will enable teachers and parents to provide the optimal conditions for successful learning.

Sample questionnaire: LSA-Senior

Please note: This is not a test, there are NO trick questions, no 'right' or 'wrong' answers. Mark only statements that are really true for you!

Name:_____ Class:_____

Mark only statements that are really true for you!

1A __I really need it quiet when I concentrate.
__When I study or read I have to get away from noise and distractions.
__Traffic noise, music, the TV and talking reduces my concentration.
☐ __People around me, who talk and move, really bother me when I study or read.

For successful curriculum delivery teachers need reliable information about their students' learning styles. This knowledge is provided through LSA instruments for different age groups which give detailed information about biological (natural) and learned (conditioned) learning needs. Familiarity with LSA results is a necessary and most effective teaching tool for educators.

Application

The response time for each questionnaire is 20-30 minutes, dependent on the age group and reading level of the student.

Plan and implement a well-organized introduction to LSA. To achieve the most reliable results it is important that you explain to students how to respond. Point out that this is not a test, that there are no 'right' or 'wrong' answers and that nobody can ever fail.

Students need to understand that the LSA profile will give them some important ideas about becoming a more successful learner and the result will also help the school and their teachers adjust their teaching methods and learning environment to help students learn better.

Give your students the following instructions before doing online LSAs:

1. Think about when you are learning something new and/or difficult.
2. Click on all statements that apply to you.
3. Answer as quickly as possible, there's no need to ponder on each statement.
4. If you need to, take a stretch during the time you are working on the computer, just be careful and don't disturb anyone else.
5. Answer quickly and appropriately. No cheating – the computer programme will catch you out!
6. Your honest results will help both you and us!
7. Ask the students: 'Are there any questions?'

TIP:
With young students do the first few questions together or read them all out loud. Do *not* prompt but offer your help during this activity, allowing them to ask questions if they have problems responding.

Information

LSA instruments

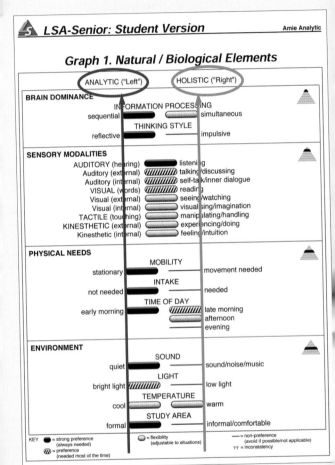

LSA-Senior: Student Version *Amie Analytic*

Graph 1. Natural / Biological Elements

ANALYTIC ("Left")   HOLISTIC ("Right")

BRAIN DOMINANCE

INFORMATION PROCESSING
sequential — simultaneous

THINKING STYLE
reflective — impulsive

SENSORY MODALITIES

AUDITORY (hearing) listening
Auditory (external) talking/discussing
Auditory (internal) self-talk/inner dialogue
VISUAL (words) reading
Visual (external) seeing/watching
Visual (internal) visualising/imagination
TACTILE (touching) manipulating/handling
KINESTHETIC (external) experiencing/doing
Kinesthetic (internal) feeling/intuition

PHYSICAL NEEDS

MOBILITY
stationary — movement needed

INTAKE
not needed — needed

TIME OF DAY
early morning — late morning
afternoon
evening

ENVIRONMENT

SOUND
quiet — sound/noise/music

LIGHT
bright light — low light

TEMPERATURE
cool — warm

STUDY AREA
formal — informal/comfortable

KEY = strong preference (always needed)   = flexibility (adjustable to situations)   — = non-preference (avoid if possible/not applicable)
  = preference (needed most of the time)   ?? = inconsistency

Explanation

The opposite page shows examples of Creative Learning Centre computerized LSA profiles, developed since 1992 and available on the internet. They are based on the original Dunn and Dunn Learning Style Model, which was created in the USA during the early 1970s. Expanded and reshaped, the LSA allows students to find out what their preferred learning conditions are and how they function best when they have to learn something new and/or difficult. Parent and teacher versions give guidelines for supporting students in their learning in class and at home.

All instruments have the same look and format, consisting of a cover page, a profile summary, a personal report, graph 1: biologically based elements, graph 2: conditioned/learned elements and graph 3: learning style tendencies.

Profile interpretations

To interpret the graphs in the LSA profile, the personal report gives detailed information about preferences, flexibilities, non-preferences and inconsistencies of a student's learning style. Each report is self-explanatory but for further in-depth explanations and practical applications in the classroom there is also an LSA Interpretation Manual available from www.creativelearningcentre.com.

As teachers often don't have time to interpret all individual LSA profiles of their students, there are group profiles available at no extra cost and the same guidelines as for interpreting individual profiles apply.

Although it is important to interpret individual elements of a student's profile, it is even more important to understand style combinations because they give insight into students' behaviour and learning capabilities as well as explanations for underachievement or learning success.

Information

LSA profile summary

The LSA profile summary page gives a quick overview of all the preferences and non-preferences of a student, describing how they can learn best and what they need to avoid when concentrating on something new and/or difficult. Flexibilities are not included in this summary.

 LSA-Junior: Student Version

Profile Summary

Melissa, now you know how you learn best (through your preferences).
When you can use your preferences at school and doing your homework,
you will be more successful.
However, when you have to use your non-preferences you will find learning harder.
And you may not feel happy about working this way.
This may lead to you not liking school and getting marks or grades that don't show how
smart you really are.
It's best if you are allowed to **learn YOUR way** - in school, at home and later in life.
The following pages describe in detail how you learn best.
Discuss your profile with your teachers and the grown-ups in your family.

Key points (elements) of my style
when I have to learn something NEW and/or DIFFICULT:

My Preferences: (How I learn best)

THINKING:

All-at-once (simultaneous Information Processing)
I like to do many things at the same time, otherwise it's boring.

Think-First Style (reflective)
I like to think about something before doing it.

SENSES:

Watching (visual - external)
I need to see how things are done; I like watching people and everything around me.

Action (kinesthetic, doing/experiencing)
I like to go on field trips, do things in class, and act out stories.

Feelings (kinesthetic internal/intuition)
I need to feel good about the things we're studying.

PHYSICAL NEEDS:

Butterflies (late morning preference)
My concentration is best in the time just before lunch.

Night Owls (evening preference)
I like learning when it's time to go to bed.

CLASSROOM AND HOME: none

SOCIAL: none

ATTITUDES: none

My Non-Preferences: (What does not help my learning)

THINKING:

Step-By-Step (sequential Information Processing)
Doing several things at the same time confuses me.

SENSES:

Self-talk (auditory - internal)
I never talk to myself. Talking in my head is not for me.

Interpretation

The introduction to the profile summary page gives explanations about the difference between preferences (how a student can learn best) and non-preferences (what makes it harder for a student to learn something difficult). The advice is to encourage students to learn 'their way' – in school, at home and later in life – as well as to discuss their results with teachers and parents.

The key points on the profile summary page of the LSA-Student version give a pictorial overview with very simple explanations of all elements of the LS model, showing preferences or non-preferences in the following six areas:

brain dominance (brain style)

sensory modalities (senses)

physical needs (including biorhythm)

environment (study area, classroom and at home)

social aspects (with whom to learn best)

attitudes towards learning.

Flexibilities are not included in the profile summary page but they can be found in the three graphs at the end of the LSA document, after the personal report.

The same goes for inconsistencies (which are represented through question marks in the LSA profile) because it is most important to concentrate on a student's strengths and how they can achieve academic success.

The results from the profile summary page can also be used with younger students, who can colour in the LSA pyramid on the cover page of the LSA instrument, highlighting all their preferences and crossing out their non-preferences. This way they can do a tactile/visual activity about their own learning style.

LSA profile: biological elements

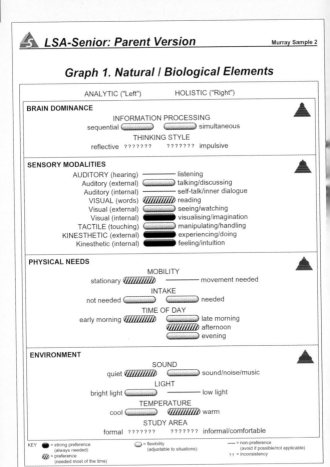

LSA-Senior: Parent Version

Murray Sample 2

Graph 1. Natural / Biological Elements

ANALYTIC ("Left")   HOLISTIC ("Right")

BRAIN DOMINANCE

INFORMATION PROCESSING
sequential ———— simultaneous
THINKING STYLE
reflective ??????? ??????? impulsive

SENSORY MODALITIES

AUDITORY (hearing) ———— listening
Auditory (external) ———— talking/discussing
Auditory (internal) ———— self-talk/inner dialogue
VISUAL (words) ———— reading
Visual (external) ———— seeing/watching
Visual (internal) ———— visualising/imagination
TACTILE (touching) ———— manipulating/handling
KINESTHETIC (external) ———— experiencing/doing
Kinesthetic (internal) ———— feeling/intuition

PHYSICAL NEEDS

MOBILITY
stationary ———— movement needed
INTAKE
not needed ———— needed
TIME OF DAY
early morning ———— late morning
———— afternoon
———— evening

ENVIRONMENT

SOUND
quiet ———— sound/noise/music
LIGHT
bright light ———— low light
TEMPERATURE
cool ———— warm
STUDY AREA
formal ??????? ??????? informal/comfortable

KEY ● = strong preference (always needed)   ○ = flexibility (adjustable to situations)   ——— = non-preference (avoid if possible/not applicable)
▨ = preference (needed most of the time)   ?? = inconsistency

Interpretation

The top four layers of the LSA pyramid represent a student's biological needs when concentrating, reading a study text, doing homework or learning something new and/or difficult. They contain the following style elements:

1. **Left/right-brain dominance**

   This element shows analytic/holistic information processing strategies, reflective or impulsive thinking styles and overall analytic or holistic/global learning style tendencies.

2. **Sensory modalities or perception**

   This includes the following preferences: auditory (hearing, talking, inner dialogue); visual (reading, seeing/watching, visualizing); tactile (manipulating, touching) and kinesthetic (doing, feeling).

3. **Physical needs**

   This element identifies preferences for mobility (moving or being stationary); intake and mouth stimulation (eating, nibbling, drinking, chewing) and time of day preferences (personal biorhythm).

4. **Environmental conditions**

   This reveals preferences for sound or quiet, low or bright light, room temperature (needing it to be cool or warm) and formal or informal/comfortable study area.

Preferences and non-preferences in these areas grow with the child and are usually hard to change, remaining mostly stable over a lifetime. Mismatched over longer periods of time, they will diminish learning motivation, persistence and responsibility for schoolwork. For lasting school success it is crucial that preferences (particularly biological preferences) are matched most of the time. They become a student's strengths and will help to develop positive attitudes towards learning.

LSA profile:
conditioned/learned elements

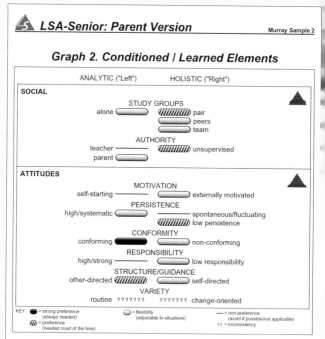

LSA-Senior: Parent Version
Murray Sample 2

Graph 2. Conditioned / Learned Elements

ANALYTIC ("Left")   HOLISTIC ("Right")

SOCIAL

STUDY GROUPS
alone — pair / peers / team

AUTHORITY
teacher — unsupervised
parent —

ATTITUDES

MOTIVATION
self-starting — externally motivated

PERSISTENCE
high/systematic — spontaneous/fluctuating / low persistence

CONFORMITY
conforming — non-conforming

RESPONSIBILITY
high/strong — low responsibility

STRUCTURE/GUIDANCE
other-directed — self-directed

VARIETY
routine ??????? ??????? change-oriented

KEY: ● = strong preference (always needed)   ○ = flexibility (adjustable to situations)   — = non-preference (avoid if possible/not applicable)
▨ = preference (needed most of the time)   ?? = inconsistency

DIFFERENCES BETWEEN BIOLOGICAL & LEARNED ELEMENTS:
The results in Graph 1 represent Murray's biological needs when concentrating, reading a study text or learning something new and difficult. Preferences and non-preferences in these areas are usually hard to change and remain mostly stable over a life time. When they are mismatched over a longer period of time they will influence learning motivation, persistence and responsibility in a negative way. For lasting learning success, make sure that his strong preferences are being matched most of the time.
The results in Graph 2 reveal his conditioning, and show with whom he learns best and what his attitudes are when it comes to learning something new and difficult. These elements are not stable in a person's profile and can change quite rapidly. This usually happens when there are changes going on inside the person or in the world around him. To be successful at school it is very important that Murray develops positive attitudes and always attempts the best he can do because his preferences will become his strengths when he uses them wisely.

Interpretation

The remaining two layers of the LSA pyramid define a student's learned or conditioned style features, particularly when faced with rules and regulations in school or at home, when working with classmates, doing homework or learning something new and/or difficult. They contain the following style elements.

5. **Social groupings**

    This element describes preferences for working alone, with a partner or classmate, with peers, or in a team, with or without an authority figure, which could be a teacher, parent or other grown-up.

6. **Attitudes**

    This identifies motivation (internally or externally motivated for learning); persistence (high, fluctuating, or low); conformity (conforming or non-conforming/rebellious); responsibility (high or low); need for structure (being self-directed or needing guidance from others) and variety (needing routine or wanting change and variety).

Results in this area reveal a student's conditioning in learning attitudes, how they react to 'the system' and with whom they learn best. However, these elements are not stable, changing several times over a lifetime. They can also change quite rapidly, often depending on circumstances or even daily moods. When a lot is happening inside a student's mind or profound changes are going on around a student (family break-up, moving house, a new baby or death in the family, stress, neglect or violence) there will often be several question marks.

They often indicate that the student is under pressure and, as long as these conditions last, will have problems learning well and concentrating as normal. In such a situation support from teachers and trusted adults is most important for the well-being of the student.

LSA profile interpretations

Information

LSA profile: learning style tendencies

 LSA-Senior: Parent Version   Gretchen Gifted

Graph 3. Learning Style Tendencies

Compare this result with your Left/Right Brain Dominance in Graph 1

ANALYTIC ("Left")		HOLISTIC ("Right")
quiet		sound/noise/music
bright light		low light
formal study area		informal study area
high persistence		low persistence
no/low intake		intake needed

Three or more of the following elements: preferring quiet, bright light, formal design/work area, high persistence (to complete tasks without interruptions) and low need for intake tends to suggest an ANALYTICAL (sequential) learning style. On the other hand, preferring sound, soft lighting, informal design, low persistence (completing tasks in bursts while working on multiple tasks simultaneously) and need for intake suggests a GLOBAL/HOLISTIC (simultaneous) learning style (Bruno, 1988; Dunn, Cavanaugh, Eberle, and Zenhausern, 1982).

Left/right-brain dominance

 LSA-Senior: Parent Version   Gretchen Gift

Graph 1. Natural / Biological Elements

ANALYTIC ("Left")	HOLISTIC ("Right")

BRAIN DOMINANCE

INFORMATION PROCESSING
sequential ———————— simultaneous

THINKING STYLE
reflective ———————— impulsive

Information gained from the LSA instruments is very detailed and explains not only overall learning style tendencies but also gives in-depth information about style combinations of individual students. Teachers and parents need to know their preferences and flexibilities but, more importantly, their non-preferences, which can often become learning killers.

Interpretation

Graph 3 reveals overall tendencies in a student's learning style. Research has shown that three or more preferences in the following elements: quiet, bright light, a formal study area, high persistence and no need for intake tend to suggest an **analytical** (sequential, reflective, left-brain dominant) learning style. In contrast, preferences for the following elements: sound, soft lighting, an informal study area, low persistence and the need for intake suggest a **holistic** (simultaneous, impulsive, right-brain dominant) learning style, which most underachievers and problem students have. These results can be compared to those in graph 1, which indicated left- or right-brain dominanance.

This valuable information enables teachers and parents to understand how children and adult learners will approach learning situations and solve problems: either in a logical, detailed fashion or in a more feeling-based way, disregarding logic and sequence. Both ways are equally valuable, but in traditional education students are expected to learn analytically and those who cannot think and function in this way nearly always encounter problems because they are different, often described as underachievers. It is important that teachers learn to accommodate both styles in their teaching strategies so neither group is disadvantaged.

Preferences in both left- and right-brain areas indicate that the person is highly integrated and capable of using both brain hemispheres equally strongly. Flexibilities in these two categories indicate that the person finds it easy to switch between these different modes if necessary, which can be of great advantage.

Information

Analytic LS preferences

All graphs in the LSA profiles have a layout to indicate correlations between individual style elements and an overall analytic or holistic learning style.

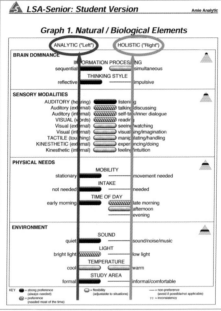

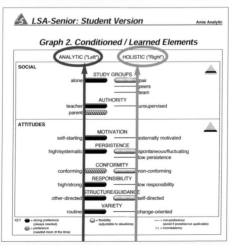

Explanation

Although people are a complex mix of style components, most have an overall preference towards one left- or right-brain dominance; only a minority is very flexible.

Preferences (combined with flexibilities) on the left-hand side of graphs 1 and 2 indicate an overall analytic learning style, which is of great advantage when students want to undertake academic studies. As traditional education institutions still mainly use frontal teaching with lectures, worksheets and textbooks, a lot of reading, discussing and work on computers, students with analytic approaches to learning, detail orientation, reflective thinking and step-by-step logic combined with the ability to work alone have an undeniable advantage and usually do well academically.

Further analysis usually shows that these students have a matched style in their physical needs: a traditional environment to study in (quiet, formal, under bright light). They also have an attitude combination that often makes them high achievers (strong persistence, responsibility, high learning motivation with need for guidance, working well with routine and conforming to rules).

Even in the sensory areas analytical students have an advantage because there is also a correlation in this area. It is not as strong as in other elements, but still noticeable. Preferences in auditory (hearing, listening, discussing) and visual words (reading) are certainly abilities that ensure academic success. These style features are the domain of theoretical learners who often learn for learning's sake. There is nothing wrong with that as long as it is not made the norm for learning in general.

Information

Holistic LS preferences

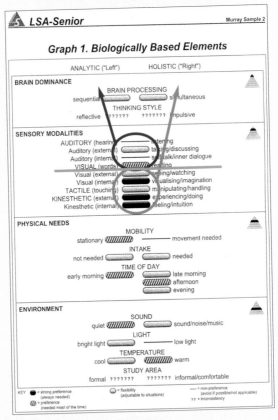

LSA-Senior · Murray Sample 2

Graph 1. Biologically Based Elements

ANALYTIC ("Left")   HOLISTIC ("Right")

BRAIN DOMINANCE

BRAIN PROCESSING
sequential / simultaneous

THINKING STYLE
reflective ?????? ??????? impulsive

SENSORY MODALITIES

AUDITORY (hearing) — listening
Auditory (external) — talking/discussing
Auditory (internal) — self talk/inner dialogue
VISUAL (words) — reading
Visual (external) — seeing/watching
Visual (internal) — visualising/imagination
TACTILE (touching) — manipulating/handling
KINESTHETIC (external) — experiencing/doing
Kinesthetic (internal) — feeling/intuition

PHYSICAL NEEDS

MOBILITY
stationary — movement needed

INTAKE
not needed — needed

TIME OF DAY
early morning — late morning
afternoon
evening

ENVIRONMENT

SOUND
quiet — sound/noise/music

LIGHT
bright light — low light

TEMPERATURE
cool — warm

STUDY AREA
formal ?????? ?????? informal/comfortable

KEY: ● = strong preference (always needed) · ◯ = flexibility (adjustable to situations) · ///// = preference (needed most of the time) · — = non-preference (avoid if possible/not applicable) · ?? = inconsistency

It is interesting to note that the division between analytic and holistic correlations in the sensory modalities goes right through the visual elements (between visual words – reading and visual external – seeing/watching). If a student does not have preferences above the green line but strong preferences below, particularly in kinesthetic, as in this example, there will be problems in academic learning. The reason is that traditional teaching does not cater for these non-academic learning needs and the student cannot learn successfully through listening, reading and discussing. This causes negative feelings about learning and unwillingness to participate.

Explanation

Preferences (combined with flexibilities) on the right-hand side in graphs 1 and 2 indicate an overall holistic learning style, which is generally a disadvantage when students want to undertake academic studies in traditional learning institutions. As these students do not use analytic approaches to learning, get bored by reflective and step-by-step logic because they are spontaneous, creative and sociable, they are the typical non-academic learners, often not completing their studies or changing subjects.

Through other holistic correlations of their preferences, these students also have a mismatched style between their physical needs and the traditional environment they have to study in. They often prefer music, informal seating in low light and have an attitude combination that makes them non-conformists and rebels. They show fluctuating persistence, low responsibility, need external learning motivation, have little tolerance for routine and don't want structure. Often, they are against authority, socialize while they study and dislike conforming to rules. None of these attitudes are rewarded by teachers or educational systems.

Holistic students have a particular disadvantage in the sensory area because there is also a correlation there – not as strong as in the bipolar elements, but still noticeable. Non-preferences in auditory (listening, discussing) and visual words (text reading) certainly contribute to academic failure. In addition, holistic students' 'non-academic' styles of tactile and kinesthetic learning needs (hands-on and experiencing) are a distinct hindrance and their need to visualize finds an outlet in daydreaming when they are bored with their studies.

Flexible LSA profile

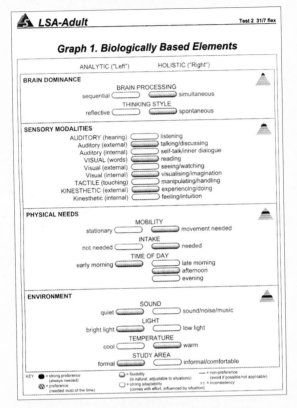

If a student has only flexibilities or adaptabilities but no preferences or non-preferences in their profile, then the Summary Page will look very different without key elements, but the profile is still valid.

Key elements of my learning style
when I have to learn something NEW and/or DIFFICULT:

My Preferences: (how I learn best)

BRAIN DOMINANCE:	none
SENSORY MODALITIES:	none
PHYSICAL NEEDS:	none
ENVIRONMENT:	none
SOCIAL:	none
ATTITUDES:	none

My Non-Preferences: (what I need to avoid when learning something difficult)

BRAIN DOMINANCE:	none
SENSORY MODALITIES:	none
PHYSICAL NEEDS:	none
ENVIRONMENT:	none
SOCIAL:	none
ATTITUDES:	none

Interpretation

Flexibility or adaptability means that the student can naturally adjust to changing situations and adapt their style as required. This is a great advantage in some areas, such as physical needs, the environment or in social groupings, but might be a disadvantage in some other areas.

Flexibilities are the unstable elements in a person's profile and are not included in the summary page. They can and will change, particularly in the sensory areas, either to preferences, when a student is interested, or to non-preferences when the interest disappears. Our research has shown the more flexibility a student has in the senses, the more fluctuation there will be in their academic performance. As long as students are **interested** in the content and **motivated** to learn, they will do so with good outcomes.

But: when they lose interest they will switch off and might even pretend not to understand so they don't have to participate. This is often the case with underachievers and is puzzling to teachers. Once they understand LS combinations, teachers will have more success in supporting their students and drawing out their true learning potential.

Being flexible in brain dominance means that one can be either quick and spontaneous or reflective and slower in responding to questions and problems. The advantage is that flexible thinkers can naturally adjust their thinking style to match the situation. Given the complexity of modern home and school life, it is almost necessary to be highly flexible in one's thinking style. Being strongly holistic or strictly analytic, mainly reflective or always spontaneous will not help students to cope with learning situations and might cause problems later in their work life.

Information

LSA group results – preferences

LSA-Senior — 15 Seniors - Group Profile

prepared for: Network Educational Press 22/02/04	15 Seniors - Group Profile Chris Dickinson Total number in group = 15

Group Percentages I (preferences)

Graph shows the % of people with preferences in the following areas

	Left preference	%		%	Right preference
INFORMATION PROCESSING	sequential	33		13	simultaneous
THINKING STYLE	reflective	26		20	impulsive
SENSORY MODALITIES	AUDITORY (hearing)			60	listening
	Auditory (external)			66	talking/discussing
	Auditory (internal)			66	self-talk/inner dialogue
	VISUAL (words)			66	reading
	Visual (external)			73	seeing/watching
	Visual (internal)			60	visualising/imagination
	TACTILE (touching)			66	manipulating/handling
	KINESTHETIC (external)			66	experiencing/doing
	Kinesthetic (internal)			60	feeling/intuition
MOBILITY	stationary	40		13	movement needed
INTAKE	not needed	6		73	needed
TIME OF DAY	early morning	26		53	late morning
				33	afternoon
				26	evening
SOUND	quiet	33		33	sound/noise/music
LIGHT	bright light	33		13	low light
TEMPERATURE	cool	6		46	warm
STUDY AREA	formal	40		26	informal/comfortable
STUDY GROUPS	alone	6		53	pair
				53	peers
				60	team
AUTHORITY	teacher	6		6	unsupervised
	parent	26			
MOTIVATION	self-starting	66		0	externally motivated
PERSISTENCE	high/systematic	46		13	spontaneous/fluctuating
				13	low persistence
CONFORMITY	conforming	40		13	non-conforming
RESPONSIBILITY	high/strong	40		13	low responsibility
STRUCT/GUIDANCE	other-directed	60		6	self-directed
VARIETY	routine	13		53	change-oriented
LS Tendencies	analytic	20		6	holistic/global

KEY ▬ = preferences

Interpretation

The key to an easy and successful introduction of LS to the classroom is to look for extreme results (strong preferences and non-preferences), subgroup students with similar needs and implement whatever strategies can be used to accommodate different styles. This means teachers don't necessarily need to cater for everyone's individual needs, but any actions they take to match teaching and learning styles will benefit the learning process, particularly when students are confronted with something new and/or difficult.

The chart on the facing page shows the percentages of students with preferences compiled from their individual personal LSA profiles. If a teacher has a minimum of five individual LSA profiles stored in their web account they can very simply create any number of group profiles without extra cost.

Preference results above 60 per cent are significant and must be considered when devising effective teaching strategies. Try to accommodate these learning needs whenever you can. For instance, if 85 per cent of your students learn best through feeling/intuition, 75 per cent need authority and 68 per cent need time to visualize what they have heard, seen or read, your teaching strategies need to allow for that by making your students feel good the moment they enter your classroom and by presenting learning content in a way that makes sense to them. It also means that you need to exercise your authority in a positive, non-threatening way to avoid negative feelings that will certainly switch off students with such preferences.

Information

LSA group results – non-preferences

 LSA-Senior

15 Seniors - Group Profile

prepared for:
Network Educational Press
22/02/04

15 Seniors - Group Profile
Chris Dickinson
Total number in group = 15

Group Percentages II (non-preferences)

Graph shows the % of people with non-preferences in the following areas

INFORMATION PROCESSING	sequential	0	0	simultaneous
THINKING STYLE	reflective	20 ——	— 13	impulsive
SENSORY MODALITIES	AUDITORY (hearing)		— 13	listening
	Auditory (external)		– 6	talking/discussing
	Auditory (internal)		0	self-talk/inner dialogue
	VISUAL (words)		– 6	reading
	Visual (external)		0	seeing/watching
	Visual (internal)		0	visualising/imagination
	TACTILE (touching)		0	manipulating/handling
	KINESTHETIC (external)		– 6	experiencing/doing
	Kinesthetic (internal)		0	feeling/intuition
MOBILITY	stationary	26 ——	– 6	movement needed
INTAKE	not needed	33 ——	– 6	needed
TIME OF DAY	early morning	26 ——	— 13	late morning
			— 20	afternoon
			—— 26	evening
SOUND	quiet	20 ——	—— 26	sound/noise/music
LIGHT	bright light	0	——— 46	low light
TEMPERATURE	cool	6 –	0	warm
STUDY AREA	formal	20 ——	– 6	informal/comfortable
STUDY GROUPS	alone	40 ———	— 13	pair
			– 13	peers
			– 6	team
AUTHORITY	teacher	6 –	— 13	unsupervised
	parent	6 –		
MOTIVATION	self-starting	0	——— 46	externally motivated
PERSISTENCE	high/systematic	13 —	0	spontaneous/fluctuating
			——— 33	low persistence
CONFORMITY	conforming	0	– 6	non-conforming
RESPONSIBILITY	high/strong	6 –	— 20	low responsibility
STRUCT/GUIDANCE	other-directed	0	– 6	self-directed
VARIETY	routine	13 —	0	change-oriented
LS Tendencies	analytic	13 —	0	holistic/global

KEY —— = non-preferences

Interpretation

The graph opposite shows the percentage of students with non-preferences in a group compiled from their individual personal LSA profiles.

In this section, results **above 40 per cent** are significant. These elements should be **avoided** whenever possible.

Look into the areas of high scores (above 40 per cent) and try to avoid teaching through these strategies whenever possible (except in 'Attitudes' where it can also mean that these elements are not applicable for some students).

For example, if 37 per cent of your students do not learn well by listening, 55 per cent find it difficult to concentrate in the afternoon and 43 per cent do not like to learn when they are unsupervised, then these must be avoided. If it is not possible to avoid teaching through your students' non-preferences, make sure that as many of their other learning preferences as possible are matched.

Non-preferences become weaknesses the longer a student has to use them when confronted with something new and/or difficult. This can lead to frustration for all concerned, but inevitably to concentration problems, low motivation and ultimately learning difficulties. Many students who are termed problem students, underachievers or identified as having special needs could learn very well if they were allowed to learn through their preferences, which are actually their strengths.

TIP:

Accept that students learn in many different ways. Even if the way they want to learn doesn't make sense to you as their teacher, respect their individuality and support them as much as possible in their sometimes 'weird' learning style. The rewards will be swift and profound!

LSA group results – flexibilities

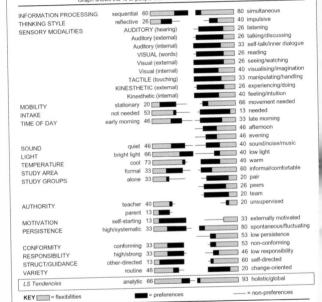

 LSA-Senior   15 Seniors - Group Profile

prepared for:
Network Educational Press
22/02/04

15 Seniors - Group Profile
Chris Dickinson
Total number in group = 15

Group Percentages III (flexibilities)

Graph shows the % of people with flexibilities in the following areas

Category	Left	%		Right
INFORMATION PROCESSING	sequential	60		80 simultaneous
THINKING STYLE	reflective	26		40 impulsive
SENSORY MODALITIES	AUDITORY (hearing)			26 listening
	Auditory (external)			26 talking/discussing
	Auditory (internal)			33 self-talk/inner dialogue
	VISUAL (words)			26 reading
	Visual (external)			26 seeing/watching
	Visual (internal)			40 visualising/imagination
	TACTILE (touching)			33 manipulating/handling
	KINESTHETIC (external)			26 experiencing/doing
	Kinesthetic (internal)			40 feeling/intuition
MOBILITY	stationary	20		66 movement needed
INTAKE	not needed	53		13 needed
TIME OF DAY	early morning	46		33 late morning
				46 afternoon
				46 evening
SOUND	quiet	46		40 sound/noise/music
LIGHT	bright light	66		40 low light
TEMPERATURE	cool	73		40 warm
STUDY AREA	formal	33		60 informal/comfortable
STUDY GROUPS	alone	33		20 pair
				26 peers
				20 team
AUTHORITY	teacher	40		20 unsupervised
	parent	13		
MOTIVATION	self-starting	13		33 externally motivated
PERSISTENCE	high/systematic	33		80 spontaneous/fluctuating
				53 low persistence
CONFORMITY	conforming	33		53 non-conforming
RESPONSIBILITY	high/strong	33		46 low responsibility
STRUCT/GUIDANCE	other-directed	13		60 self-directed
VARIETY	routine	46		20 change-oriented
LS Tendencies	analytic	66		93 holistic/global

KEY ☐ = flexibilities   ■ = preferences   ----- = non-preferences

Interpretation

Flexibilities are an important asset for a student to have in their overall LSA profile. In most areas flexibilities are a great advantage, but not in all (see page 25).

To work with the results in Graph III, showing flexibilities in the percentage figures, some arithmetic is necessary.

1. Add together the percentages of **preferences** and **flexibilities** Graphs I and III – always using the same LSA element, for example intake or formal study area, sound or mobility.

2. Check which results are **above 80 per cent** – these *must* be considered important for the majority of students in this group. Teachers are always surprised at the number of areas in which nearly *all* their students have similar needs – but this is a factor that actually makes personalized teaching to groups possible. Without LSA, however, many learning needs remain hidden.

3. Incorporate appropriate teaching methods (for example tactile and kinesthetic techniques, use of music, allowing students to move around while working, teaching new and difficult content in the morning if possible, and so on).

4. Subgroup students by consulting the page in the group results where each student's full profile is listed and where teachers can easily see which students should be grouped together.

Once students understand how Group Profiles work, they learn to subgroup themselves, particularly older students who are much less teacher-dependent.

> **TIP:**
> For more detailed interpretation of flexibilities teachers can consult the LSA Interpretation Manual, available online at: www.creativelearningcentre.com/default.asp?page=lsat

LSA group profile – question marks

LSA-Senior

15 Seniors - Group Profile

Group Results

Chris Dickinson

Group member code number		1	2	3	4	5	6	7	8	9	10	11	12	13	14	15	
INFORMATION PROCESSING	sequential	⊘	⊘	●	⊘	◐	◐	??	⊘	◐	◐	⊘	⊘	●	●	◐	sequential (analytic)
	simultaneous	◐	◐	◐	◐	◐	◐	??	◐	◐	◐	◐	◐	◐	◐	◐	simultaneous (holistic)
THINKING STYLE	reflective	—	⊘	??	◐	◐	●	●	??	◐	—	—	●	??	??	◐	reflective
	impulsive	◐	◐	—	??	◐	◐	—	◐	??	◐	◐	◐	??	??	◐	impulsive
SENSES	AUDITORY (hearing)	◐	⊘	⊘	●	◐	◐	◐	⊘	—	◐	◐	◐	◐	●	●	listening
	Auditory (external)	◐	⊘	⊘	●	●	◐	⊘	⊘	—	◐	◐	●	●	●	●	talking/discussing
	Auditory (internal)	⊘	◐	⊘	●	●	◐	◐	●	●	◐	◐	◐	◐	●	●	self-talk/inner dialogue
	VISUAL (words)	◐	◐	●	◐	●	◐	⊘	⊘	⊘	⊘	—	◐	◐	●	●	reading
	Visual (external)	◐	◐	◐	●	◐	◐	◐	◐	◐	◐	—	◐	◐	●	●	seeing/watching
	Visual (internal)	●	●	◐	◐	◐	◐	◐	●	●	◐	●	●	◐	◐	◐	visualising/imagination
	TACTILE (touching)	●	●	●	◐	◐	◐	⊘	◐	◐	◐	◐	●	●	●	●	manipulating/handling
	KINESTHETIC (external)	⊘	⊘	⊘	◐	◐	◐	◐	◐	●	◐	◐	●	●	●	●	experiencing/doing
	Kinesthetic (internal)	●	●	◐	◐	◐	●	●	●	●	●	◐	◐	●	●	●	feeling/intuition
MOBILITY	stationary	⊘	●	●	◐	—	—	◐	◐	◐	??	◐	—	◐	??	●	stationary
	movement needed	◐	◐	—	◐	◐	◐	◐	◐	◐	??	●	●	◐	??	◐	movement needed
INTAKE	not needed	◐	◐	◐	●	◐	◐	◐	◐	◐	??	—	◐	—	—	●	not needed
	needed	◐	◐	—	●	●	●	●	◐	◐	??	◐	◐	◐	◐	◐	needed
TIME OF DAY	early morning	◐	◐	◐	●	◐	◐	◐	◐	◐	—	⊘	◐	◐	◐	●	early morning
	late morning	—	⊘	◐	◐	◐	⊘	◐	◐	◐	—	◐	◐	⊘	◐	◐	late morning
	afternoon	◐	◐	◐	◐	◐	—	◐	⊘	◐	—	⊘	—	◐	●	◐	afternoon
	evening	◐	◐	◐	◐	◐	◐	◐	●	◐	—	◐	◐	◐	◐	●	evening
SOUND	quiet	◐	⊘	◐	◐	◐	◐	◐	◐	—	◐	—	◐	◐	●	●	quiet
	sound/noise/music	◐	◐	◐	◐	◐	◐	◐	◐	◐	◐	—	⊘	◐	◐	●	sound/noise/music
LIGHT	bright light	◐	◐	⊘	◐	◐	⊘	◐	◐	◐	◐	◐	⊘	⊘	⊘	●	bright light
	low light	—	—	◐	◐	◐	◐	◐	◐	⊘	—	—	●	●	◐	◐	low light
TEMPERATURE	cool	◐	◐	◐	◐	◐	??	??	◐	—	●	—	⊘	◐	◐	◐	cool
	warm	◐	◐	◐	◐	◐	??	??	◐	—	●	—	◐	◐	◐	◐	warm
STUDY AREA	formal	⊘	⊘	◐	◐	◐	◐	??	●	●	●	—	◐	◐	●	◐	formal
	informal/comfortable	◐	◐	—	◐	◐	—	??	◐	◐	◐	◐	⊘	⊘	◐	◐	informal/comfortable
STUDY GROUPS	alone	—	—	◐	◐	??	—	—	—	◐	●	◐	—	◐	??	??	alone
	pair	◐	◐	◐	●	—	⊘	◐	◐	◐	◐	—	⊘	◐	??	??	pair
	peers	●	●	◐	⊘	—	◐	◐	◐	◐	◐	◐	◐	◐	??	??	peers
	team	●	◐	⊘	—	◐	●	◐	??	??	◐	●	◐	◐	??	??	team
AUTHORITY	teacher	◐	◐	⊘	??	◐	◐	◐	⊘	??	—	??	??	??	??	??	teacher
	unsupervised	??	—	◐	??	—	??	◐	◐	??	◐	??	??	??	??	??	unsupervised
	parent	??	??	◐	??	◐	—	??	??	??	??	??	??	??	??	??	parent
MOTIVATION	self-starting	◐	●	●	●	◐	—	??	●	◐	??	◐	◐	●	??	◐	self-starting
	externally motivated	◐	—	—	—	◐	◐	◐	—	◐	◐	??	◐	●	??	◐	externally motivated
PERSISTENCE	high/systematic	⊘	●	●	◐	◐	—	??	●	●	◐	◐	◐	◐	◐	◐	high/systematic
	spontaneous/fluctuating	◐	◐	◐	◐	◐	⊘	??	◐	◐	◐	◐	◐	◐	◐	◐	spontaneous/fluctuating
	low persistence	—	—	◐	◐	◐	◐	??	◐	◐	◐	◐	⊘	◐	●	◐	low persistence
CONFORMITY	conforming	??	⊘	●	◐	⊘	◐	◐	??	●	◐	●	◐	◐	◐	??	conforming
	non-conforming	??	◐	◐	??	◐	◐	◐	??	◐	??	◐	⊘	⊘	◐	??	non-conforming
RESPONSIBILITY	high/strong	◐	◐	●	●	●	●	??	⊘	◐	●	◐	◐	◐	●	??	high/strong
	low responsibility	⊘	—	—	◐	◐	—	??	??	◐	◐	●	●	◐	●	??	low responsibility
STRUCT/GUIDANCE	other-directed	●	●	●	●	●	??	●	◐	⊘	??	??	??	●	◐	??	other-directed
	self-directed	●	●	●	◐	◐	??	◐	⊘	—	??	??	??	●	◐	??	self-directed
VARIETY	routine	◐	◐	??	●	●	◐	—	??	◐	??	—	◐	◐	??	◐	routine
	change-oriented	◐	—	??	◐	●	●	●	??	●	??	⊘	⊘	●	??	◐	change-oriented

KEY ● strong preference   ⊘ preference   — non-preference   ◯ flexibility   ?? inconsistency

Interpretation

The page opposite shows an LSA group profile, showing every single LS element of each individual student in a group.

The more question marks that are visible in a personal profile, the more it is likely that the student:

■ is under stress;

■ is currently experiencing confusion;

■ is undergoing change in these areas;

■ has reading problems or was confused about the questionnaire (which occurs very rarely).

As question marks always indicate some kind of problem (most often due to family difficulties or traumatic experiences in the student's life), they are reliable gauges of stress a student is experiencing.

This can lead to behaviour problems, loss of motivation, learning difficulties, underachievement, despair and ultimately dropping out of formal education. It is important that teachers talk to the student about these areas in their LSA profile and attempt to find out the reasons for these inconsistencies. It's a great help for counselling to start with question mark areas.

Students' names aren't revealed on this page for reasons of anonymity. They can be correlated from information given separately in the group profile that reveals all the students' names, gender, age and when the LSA profile was generated. To help teachers with analytic and/or holistic approaches, square or round symbols have been placed in front of the names of students who show strong overall tendencies in these areas. Students without these symbols are flexible and can be subgrouped in many different ways (see page 31).

Analytic/holistic group results

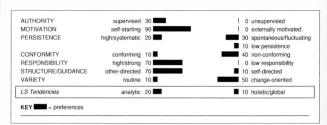

AUTHORITY	supervised 30		0 unsupervised
MOTIVATION	self-starting 90		0 externally motivated
PERSISTENCE	high/systematic 20		30 spontaneous/fluctuating
			10 low persistence
CONFORMITY	conforming 10		40 non-conforming
RESPONSIBILITY	high/strong 70		0 low responsibility
STRUCTURE/GUIDANCE	other-directed 70		10 self-directed
VARIETY	routine 10		50 change-oriented
LS Tendencies	analytic 20		10 holistic/global

KEY ▬ = preferences

LSA-Adult group

AUTHORITY	supervised 30		10 unsupervised
MOTIVATION	self-starting 100		0 externally motivated
PERSISTENCE	high/systematic 40		0 spontaneous/fluctuating
			0 low persistence
CONFORMITY	conforming 30		50 non-conforming
RESPONSIBILITY	high/strong 80		0 low responsibility
STRUCTURE	other-directed 40		20 self-directed
VARIETY	routine 10		60 change-oriented
WS Tendencies	analytic 50		0 holistic/global

KEY ▬ = preferences

WSA group (employees)

AUTHORITY	teacher 30		30 unsupervised
	parent 30		
MOTIVATION	self-starting 10		50 externally motivated
PERSISTENCE	high/systematic 50		10 spontaneous/fluctuating
			40 low persistence
CONFORMITY	conforming 30		0 non-conforming
RESPONSIBILITY	high/strong 30		10 low responsibility
STRUCTURE	other-directed 10		10 self-directed
VARIETY	routine 40		10 change-oriented
LS Tendencies	analytic 40		0 holistic/global

KEY —— = non-preferences

LSA-Senior group (teenagers)

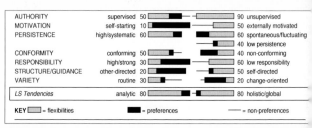

AUTHORITY	supervised 50		90 unsupervised
MOTIVATION	self-starting 10		50 externally motivated
PERSISTENCE	high/systematic 60		60 spontaneous/fluctuating
			40 low persistence
CONFORMITY	conforming 50		40 non-conforming
RESPONSIBILITY	high/strong 30		60 low responsibility
STRUCTURE/GUIDANCE	other-directed 20		50 self-directed
VARIETY	routine 30		20 change-oriented
LS Tendencies	analytic 80		80 holistic/global

KEY ▭ = flexibilities   ▬ = preferences   —— = non-preferences

LSA-Adult group

Interpretation

At the bottom of each group percentage graph is an additional line showing the analytic and holistic LS tendencies of the people in the group. This information is extremely important for team leaders, classroom teachers or anyone who works with groups in an educational or training setting. It reveals whether the group is more logical, analytical and detail-oriented, or more feeling-based, holistic and creative. This has major implications for the success or failure of a training programme, curriculum delivery and overall instructional methods used.

As teachers generally teach the way they learn best themselves, they will often not be aware that more than half of their students learn very differently and need different approaches. It's a sad truth that a mismatch between teaching methods and learning styles always leads to discipline problems, reduced academic achievement and often comes with a high social cost.

It is possible for both teachers and students to become more flexible in using analytic and holistic approaches but teachers need to lead the way by practising certain strategies.

TIP 1:

For analytic student groups
Help them to see the world from a holistic person's point of view: notice the bigger picture, avoid getting stuck in details, use spontaneity and creativity.

TIP 2:

For holistic students
Encourage them to pay attention to details, let them create lists of things they love to help them prioritize and let them follow instructions in a fun way without getting impatient.

TIP 3:

For revision
Team up students who have an opposite overall learning style.

Double tracking and subgrouping

In LS terms 'double tracking' means switching consciously from analytic teaching style to holistic strategies at regular intervals during each lesson. This way no students are left behind or need to suffer from teaching methods and explanations which do not make sense to them and switch them off.

In other words: analytic, step-by-step teaching is confusing for holistic students who need the big picture and tend to learn well when they can be emotionally and physically involved in a fear-free learning environment.

But holistic, unstructured, self-directed lessons can be very unsettling for analytic students who need routine, order and guidance in a predictable, more traditional learning environment.

Mini lectures with multisensory, analytic-holistic presentation for all students can be inserted at any time and then the double tracking continues.

LSA-Senior Group Profile III, showing flexibilities in analytic-holistic overall learning style

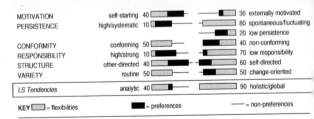

MOTIVATION	self-starting	40	30	externally motivated
PERSISTENCE	high/systematic	10	80	spontaneous/fluctuating
			20	low persistence
CONFORMITY	conforming	50	40	non-conforming
RESPONSIBILITY	high/strong	10	70	low responsibility
STRUCTURE	other-directed	40	60	self-directed
VARIETY	routine	50	50	change-oriented
LS Tendencies	analytic	40	90	holistic/global

KEY ▭ = flexibilities   ■ = preferences   —— = non-preferences

Application

Teaching analytic and holistic students simultaneously

First, students need to be subgrouped into learning groups with similar preferences.

To reach both types of students and help them become more flexible, introduce new and/or difficult curriculum content to the whole class holistically with a funny or personal story, a joke and *always* give an overview. Avoid getting lost in details!

Then let students do the following activities at the same time:

Analytic students (left-brain dominant)	Holistic students (right-brain dominant)
a. Give direct instructions, giving facts and data first (worksheets).	a. Set up a team-learning exercise with open instructions.
b. Arrange a team-learning exercise with closed questions.	b. Give facts with different multisensory learning tools.
c. Follow up with creative applications, including different learning stations.	c. Follow up with creative applications including different learning stations.
d. For revision and reinforcement, multisensory tools should be used, also role play, creative activities and learning games.	d. For revision and reinforcement, learning worksheets and writing exercises can be used, also learning games with step-by-step instructions.

Information

V-A-T-K preferences

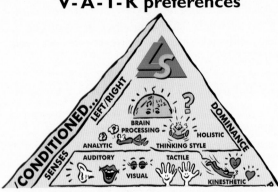

Although the **multisensory instructional approach** needs more preparation and greater teaching skills, it's the only way of keeping students engaged in the learning process, especially when curriculum content is difficult. If you want your students to remember important content, make it memorable through as many senses as possible!

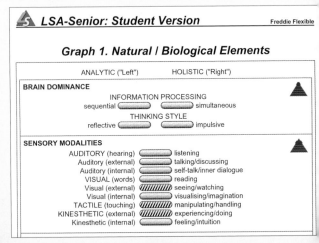

LSA-Senior: Student Version

Freddie Flexible

Graph 1. Natural / Biological Elements

	ANALYTIC ("Left")	HOLISTIC ("Right")
BRAIN DOMINANCE		▲
INFORMATION PROCESSING	sequential	simultaneous
THINKING STYLE	reflective	impulsive
SENSORY MODALITIES		▲
AUDITORY (hearing)		listening
Auditory (external)		talking/discussing
Auditory (internal)		self-talk/inner dialogue
VISUAL (words)		reading
Visual (external)		seeing/watching
Visual (internal)		visualising/imagination
TACTILE (touching)		manipulating/handling
KINESTHETIC (external)		experiencing/doing
Kinesthetic (internal)		feeling/intuition

The senses and all other biological style features can be influenced greatly by social groupings and attitudes towards school and teachers. When students don't feel good about the learning situation, they will not learn well despite the fact that they could do so if teachers would only use more interesting multisensory techniques.

Interpretation

Visual-Auditory-Tactile-Kinesthetic

All LSA instruments measure much more than VAK because in the sensory modalities area the very important distinction between tactile (hands-on) and kinesthetic (experiential/doing) learning is made – thus the term VATK. (The need for mobility is a separate element and not lumped together with kinesthetic as in regular VAK tests, as it is very different.)

Kinesthetic external refers to learning by doing, by using one's whole body, by experiencing a learning situation physically. This could include body movements to accomplish the learning task, but could also mean holding the body still and experiencing learning that way. (In contrast, when students need mobility, this means they will use body movements such as walking around, swaying, rocking or fidgeting to actually *support* learning. Although kinesthetic learners often tend to need mobility as well, it's a separate style element.)

There are also students in every class, particularly males, who often fiddle, play with their pens, tap their fingers and can't keep their hands still. Such behaviour is often interpreted by teachers as distracting, but actually means that these students are highly tactile and many will remain so for life.

In addition to the four main (external) sensory modalities, there are internal sub-modalities for auditory, visual and kinesthetic senses, which are equally important. These style features cannot be understood by merely observing students in class because information intake is extremely complicated and works through intricate combinations of sensory preferences, non-preferences and flexibilities in the human brain, influenced by the environment, physical needs, age and brain dominance of a student.

V - A - T - K non-preferences

LSA profiles show the full combination of sensory modalities in graph 1 with explanations of every element in the personal report.

earning Styles
ACTIVITY ALTERNATIVES

- A AUDITORY
speeches
debates
discussions
commentaries radio plays
panel discussions radio broadcast
interviews songs
lectures rap/chants
tape recordings jingles

KINESTHETIC - K
TV/video productions
field trips
experiential learning
demonstrations
dramatisation
experiments
role playing
pantomimes
acting
readers threatre
projects
physical activities
cross crawl
mock TV show
life theatre

ACTIVITY ALTERNATIVES

VISUAL - V
Writing
scripts
plays
poems
songs
jingles
stories
editorials
news flashes
advertisements
letters
reviews
reports
diaries
journals
Using:
pictures
filmstrips
videos
slides
OH-transparencies
magazines
newspaper clippings
crosswords
word search
coding

TACTILE - T
Making:
posters
collages
masks
puppets
costumes
mobiles
diorama
relief maps
flip chutes
electroboards
pic-a-hole
learning circles
puzzles
Using:
kooshballs
puppets
building blocks
lego
modelling clay
blind typing

T/K
Doing:
board games
floor games
dance
skits
floor shows
building
assembling

V/T
Drawing:
learning maps
wrap-arounds
pictures
graphs
charts
cartoons
murals
board games
computer work
storyboards
mind maps

Note to Students
Choose one of the activity alternatives from this chart.
You may work with several or all of the alternatives at any time

Application

Although the **multisensory approach** needs more preparation and greater teaching skills, it keeps students engaged in the learning process, especially when curriculum content is difficult. If you want your students to remember important content, make it memorable through as many senses as possible! In my book *Learning Styles in Action* there are countless reports from practitioners in various countries describing how they incorporate VATK in their daily teaching. Guidelines for such applications can be found in every LSA report, containing detailed explanations of how students need to use and combine their senses when they learn something new and/or difficult.

Flexibility/adaptability shown in the sensory modalities means that these students remember best by engaging more than one sense and *always* need a multisensory approach. Information intake through one or two modalities only (that is through listening and/or reading alone) is not sufficient for them and they can easily switch off. As long as they are *interested*, they will retain new and difficult information, but once they lose interest, their concentration disappears and their flexibility diminishes, often turning into a non-preference.

Underachievers, in particular, have flexibilities (or non-preferences) in auditory (listening) and visual words (reading) but strong preferences in tactile (hands-on) and kinesthetic (experiencing, feeling) and often a high need for mobility and comfortable seating. Due to this style combination they will either switch off or become restless and disruptive when they lose interest because they cannot follow traditional teaching methods of 'chalk-and-talk'. If such mismatches go on for longer periods of time, they become at-risk students and then drop-outs with all the negative social consequences.

Information

Sensory group results

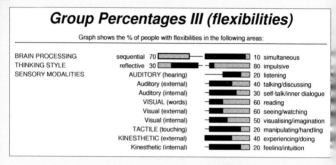

Group Percentages III (flexibilities)

Graph shows the % of people with flexibilities in the following areas:

BRAIN PROCESSING	sequential 70		10 simultaneous
THINKING STYLE	reflective 30		80 impulsive
SENSORY MODALITIES	AUDITORY (hearing)		20 listening
	Auditory (external)		40 talking/discussing
	Auditory (internal)		30 self-talk/inner dialogue
	VISUAL (words)		60 reading
	Visual (external)		60 seeing/watching
	Visual (internal)		50 visualising/imagination
	TACTILE (touching)		20 manipulating/handling
	KINESTHETIC (external)		40 experiencing/doing
	Kinesthetic (internal)		20 feeling/intuition

Creating and using self-correcting LS tools is the ultimate level of learning styles application. Any teacher not using these tools cannot rightfully claim to have introduced the full LS concept because without these tools no LS approach is complete. As only a limited range of such LS tools is commercially available, teachers, parents and students need to make their own to have new resources available, particularly to enhance learning techniques of visual/tactile students. *Learning Styles in Action* gives some instructions.

Learning Styles kit containing flip chute, earning circle, wrap around, task cards, a koosh ball and learning game.

Application

When using group profiles for preparing lessons with multisensory strategies, do the following:

1. Check which modality preference shows the largest number of students (results above 60 per cent in graph I are significant). If your students have high results in several areas, you are lucky because they can learn difficult content in different ways.

2. Double-check flexibilities in graph III to see how flexible your students are (see also page 30).

3. Also check which non-preferences your students have in the senses so that you know what to avoid for the majority of the class (see also page 28).

4. Prepare your lessons according to these findings, always catering for your students' strongest senses first, then reinforcing with their secondary strengths, then again for their flexibilities.

5. All exercises can be used and reused for all students, not at the same time for everyone but according to their preferences in sequence. In this way students' flexibilities are also trained.

6. When selecting students into sensory subgroups to teach them difficult content, consult the page with group members' names to see who can work best together when doing the same activities. (Once students are used to LS teaching they will subgroup themselves.)

7. Make sure you deliver the content in a matched style and build in exercises accommodating students' sensory preferences. When students are first exposed to new content, be aware that multisensory methods are the best approach.

> **TIP:**
> Let your students make their own LS tools, first in class and then at home with different learning content. This will help them with difficult topics.

Teaching new material through V-A-T-K

Auditory
Luke
Melissa
Robert
Sharna
Bijay
Megan
Aaron
Leah

Visual
Hayden
Rawinia
Frances
Samara
Jared
Alesha
Charlene
Danetta Elizabeth

Tactile
Kiri
Cameron
Jordan P
Michael
Bevan
Paniora
Jamie
Jade

Kinesthetic
Tyrone
Jordan K
Fomai
Nathan
John

Name lists of pupils at Forbury Primary School, Dunedin, New Zealand, displayed in class and used by their teacher to subgroup students with the same sensory preferences

Application

When teaching new and/or difficult curriculum content, LSA results give teachers invaluable information about how to subgroup students according to their preferences in the sensory modalities.

The golden rule is to let those students work together who have shown the same preferences in their LSA profile. Initially it seems like a complicated procedure, but once you are familiar with LSA group profiles and how to interpret them, it is not difficult at all. First consult the group results pages and look across the individual senses to see where the strong sensory preferences are. Then find the student names from the group members' page.

Now you have a clearer understanding about who could learn through which activities, with whom and how exercises can be done in sequence.

This is exactly what the teacher has done to create the name lists on the opposite page so that everybody knows how to begin and with whom. Even when these pupils would not normally work or play together, they will be able to relate to each other's learning because they have the same sensory needs.

Students should always be allowed to begin difficult learning tasks through their first and strongest preference. (If they have more than one, they are lucky and can start learning in several ways.) For revision they should learn through their next strongest preferences, then through their flexibilities. Only once they have understood the new content should they work through their non-preferences in order to experience a different approach and become more flexible. But nobody should have to learn new and/or difficult material through their non-preferences – it often makes learning impossible!

LSA biological style combinations

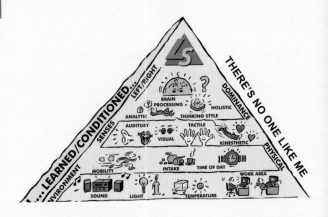

The importance of biological elements in a student's learning style cannot be underestimated because it is our biology that compels us to do certain things in certain situations, particularly under pressure.

As learning is a hugely stressful activity for many students, it is most important that teachers understand how certain combinations of style elements can lead to learning success and academic achievement or to frustration and school failure.

From research and practical experiences we know that, under pressure, flexibilities and trained style features (often learned through indoctrination) disappear. The natural/biological preferences or non-preferences gain prominence, no matter how useful or not these features might be in a difficult learning or problem-solving situation.

Interpretation

Although the elements in the four top layers of the LSA pyramid are strongly determined by natural, biological needs, they often lie hidden below years of conditioning and seem more learned than biological.

This is especially true for the combination in students' environmental learning needs. On the surface it seems that many students have a preference for quiet, bright light and formal seating and often their first-time LSA result shows these analytically correlated features. If these were their natural style preferences, these students would do well in traditional classrooms, and yet most of them struggle, find learning difficult, don't like the way they have to study, are frustrated and suffer from school stress.

Such a situation is a clear indication that they have been conditioned into learning in a certain way, mostly how teachers and parents want them to learn according to traditional beliefs. Although such conditioning processes usually go on for many years during formal schooling, they are not successful in turning these students around when they have quite different natural style features. They might, for example need sound, low light and an informal environment to learn best, often in addition to their need for mobility and intake as well as strong tactile and kinesthetic preferences. The result of such conditioning attempts is always negative, leading to loss of motivation, low self-esteem and ultimately giving up on academic learning.

Therefore it is most important for teachers not to force their students to learn in certain ways. Parents also need to understand and accept biological style combinations and let their children learn in their own unique ways.

Attitudes and social groupings

Conditioned style features

The bottom two layers of the LSA pyramid show style elements that were previously thought to be learned or conditioned because human beings are not born with abilities or knowledge in these areas. However, it seems there are also biological features as a basis for these elements, as preferences can show up very early in life, often contrary to family, social or cultural conditioning and without any training.

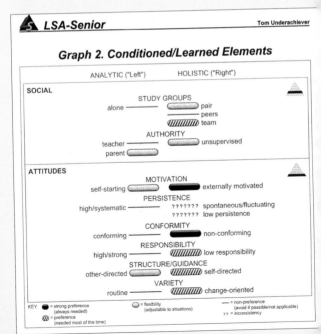

Interpretation

In contrast to the previous, biological style features in graph 1, the results in graph 2 (see example opposite) are thought to be learned and develop through conditioning from an early age. This was supported by the results of earlier research.

Over the past ten years, however, evidence has shown that at least some of these elements seem to have a biological underpinning as well. How else can it be explained that some children always need someone else around and others are better off by themselves when they have to deal with something new and/or difficult? Why do some children accept authority and others (often their siblings) don't despite upbringing in the same family? Why is it that some students show very little learning ambition, have low persistence and lack responsibility for their schoolwork despite parents and teachers helping, supporting, often pushing them?

Although these style features can be influenced at will and can change rapidly, we have also observed that certain style combinations are very stable and remain like that for many years, particularly in 'authority', 'persistence' and 'non-conformity' which can often lead to discipline problems.

LSA profiles like the one opposite display a typical style combination that can often be found among high-schools students with learning problems. It seems that no amount of training, conditioning or disciplining will bring about lasting changes in their behaviour. Yet, when these students are LSA assessed, teachers understand their learning styles and allow them to learn in their own way within the discipline framework of the school, these students become successful learners. Many teachers have experienced such positive developments and have been able to help such underachievers learn to their full potential.

Information

LS preferences of problem students

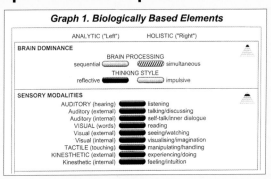

The mix of strong preferences in this section of the LSA profile reveals so called 'brain giftedness', the ability to very quickly absorb and process information in any way it comes. Unfortunately this gift does not guarantee school success.

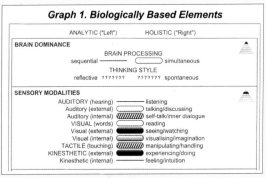

This very different combination of preferences in the same area of the LSA profile indicates difficulties in traditional learning, particularly in academic subjects as they are usually taught though lecture, discussions and reading. This does not match this student's needs for watching and experiencing new content.

When students' learning doesn't work as expected, trial and error is not much help. Teachers must know style combinations and natural learning needs of their problem students. Years of research and practical applications of LS have shown distinct style features of students who don't fit into formal classrooms and struggle academically.

Interpretation

When teachers receive their students' LSA profiles they need to look out for several important results, which are indicators for future learning failure if students continue to receive traditional, academic instruction.

Learning and behaviour problems in class can have many reasons, caused by difficult social, home and family situations but very often school failure occurs despite good intelligence, huge learning potential and every possible support a student can get. A deeper insight into the LSA results of such students has revealed combinations of LS preferences that make it extremely hard for them to become or remain successful academic learners. They might be good at sport or other non-academic subjects but struggle with the main curriculum subjects and, despite studying hard, don't have the academic success their teachers and parents expect.

By comparing thousands of LSA profiles from students in many different countries we have found that students will experience learning difficulties reaching from occasional flops to outright failure and dropping out if they:

- have a biological style combination that is unusual (like the 'brain giftedness' opposite);
- have learning needs rarely matched by the teaching style of their analytic, traditional, academic teachers (see second example opposite);
- have developed learning attitudes which are based on non-conformity due to mismatched teaching, and manifest themselves in disruptive behaviour and non-participation (see LSA graph 2 on page 48).

Teachers need to accept that they teach human beings with unique learning needs, often in overcrowded classes. Mass education has tried to deal with these issues with varying success. Underachievement and dropping out is prevalent worldwide, with all its associated social problems.

Information

Underachievers and non-academic students

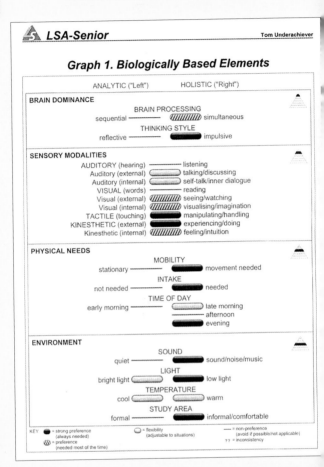

LSA-Senior
Tom Underachiever

Graph 1. Biologically Based Elements

ANALYTIC ("Left")   HOLISTIC ("Right")

BRAIN DOMINANCE

BRAIN PROCESSING
sequential ———— simultaneous

THINKING STYLE
reflective ———— impulsive

SENSORY MODALITIES

AUDITORY (hearing) ———— listening
Auditory (external) talking/discussing
Auditory (internal) self-talk/inner dialogue
VISUAL (words) ———— reading
Visual (external) seeing/watching
Visual (internal) visualising/imagination
TACTILE (touching) manipulating/handling
KINESTHETIC (external) experiencing/doing
Kinesthetic (internal) feeling/intuition

PHYSICAL NEEDS

MOBILITY
stationary ———— movement needed

INTAKE
not needed ———— needed

TIME OF DAY
early morning ———— late morning
———— afternoon
evening

ENVIRONMENT

SOUND
quiet ———— sound/noise/music

LIGHT
bright light low light

TEMPERATURE
cool warm

STUDY AREA
formal ———— informal/comfortable

KEY ● = strong preference (always needed) ◯ = flexibility (adjustable to situations) ——— = non-preference (avoid if possible/not applicable) ?? = inconsistency
▧ = preference (needed most of the time)

Long-term mismatches in biological areas lead to negative learning attitudes and behaviour problems, which can also be seen in graph 2 of the LSA (see page 48)

Interpretation

The LSA profile opposite displays the maximum number of preferences – a feature found among students who struggle with academic learning. However, not all underachievers have *all* these features in their style. In many cases as few as three or four mismatched learning needs over longer periods of time are sufficient to cause stress, frustration or despair and ultimately to switch students off from participating in the learning process in class.

In our field studies around the world we found that the following mismatched elements cause the biggest problems for students when learning something new and/or difficult, particularly during secondary education:

■ strong right-brain dominance and inability to follow sequential, logical, analytic curriculum presentation;

■ non-preference for listening to and reading about new topics, particularly when they are boring and have no practical value for students;

■ strong need for tactile and kinesthetic stimulation, which is rarely available in theoretical subjects. Without physical involvement and practical experiences understanding is impaired, interest diminishes and frustration sets in, generating negative feelings towards the subject and teacher;

■ inability to sit still for longer periods, the need for movement causing disruptive behaviour;

■ biorhythm not being matched to timetables, concentration problems during morning hours, tiredness due to staying up late as evening is preferred time;

■ preference for background music, low light and comfortable chairs, which are not available in traditional classrooms. Working in silence, under bright light with formal seating becomes physically stressful and ultimately impossible, leading to absenteeism and finally dropping out of formal education.

Underachievement based on flexibility

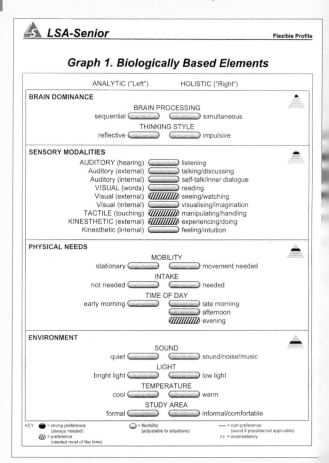

Multisensory teaching will keep flexible students interested and strengthen their flexibilities into preferences. As long as their interest and motivation for a topic last and they like the way the teacher teaches, they will learn well; if not, they will fail

Interpretation

Although a mismatch in biological learning needs and teaching styles over longer periods of time almost always leads to learning and behaviour problems, there is one other phenomenon that is particularly stressful for teachers: style flexibility in students' profiles.

The original understanding was that flexibility is good, having many flexibilities is a very useful aspect of a student's LS, giving a person additional strengths. But our field studies and reports from many practitioners have revealed that too many flexibilities can also be the reason for underachievement and academic failure.

The fact is that flexibilities in different areas of the LSA profile mean different things. They are certainly of advantage in 'physical needs' or 'environment' when easy adjustment to changing conditions is called for. They are particularly useful in 'brain dominance' where switching from one thinking style to another is certainly helpful in difficult situations.

Unfortunately, flexibility in the sensory modalities is actually a disadvantage because such students lose interest very quickly when they have to take information in through only one sense (for example auditory/listening or visual/reading) that is not their preference. To learn best they always need multisensory stimulation, otherwise they will not be able to concentrate and for flexible learners interest is the most important factor. When they are interested, they will learn very well through whichever senses, but if not, they cannot remember anything. Boredom causes their flexibilities to become non-preferences.

TIP:
Always use exercises that engage more than one sense at a time, particularly when teaching something new and/or difficult (see pages 38-45). All your students will be grateful for that and learn more!

Information

Time-of-day preferences

 ### *Learning Style* ▲*nalysis*™

Senior

prepared for:	Sample Group
7/06/01	Total number in group = 10

Group Percentages I (preferences)

Graph shows the % of people with preferences in the following areas:

BRAIN PROCESSING	sequential 10	60 simultaneous
THINKING STYLE	reflective 20	60 impulsive
SENSORY MODALITIES	AUDITORY (hearing)	20 listening
	Auditory (external)	10 talking/discussing
	Auditory (internal)	40 self-talk/inner dialogue
	VISUAL (words)	10 reading
	Visual (external)	40 seeing/watching
	Visual (internal)	30 visualising/imagination
	TACTILE (touching)	70 manipulating/handling
	KINESTHETIC (external)	40 experiencing/doing
	Kinesthetic (internal)	60 feeling/intuition

*There are significant differences in time-of-day preferences
between teenagers (LSA-Senior profile) and people in the
work place (WSA-Corporate profile), as well as in other areas*

 ### *Working Style* ▲*nalysis*™

Corporate

prepared for:	Sample Group
7/06/01	Total number in group = 10

Group Percentages I (preferences)

Graph shows the % of people with preferences in the following areas:

BRAIN PROCESSING	sequential 0	40 simultaneous
THINKING STYLE	reflective 60	10 impulsive
SENSORY MODALITIES	AUDITORY (hearing)	70 listening
	Auditory (external)	70 talking/discussing
	Auditory (internal)	10 self-talk/inner dialogue
	VISUAL (words)	40 reading
	Visual (external)	10 seeing/watching
	Visual (internal)	70 visualising/imagination
	TACTILE (touching)	20 manipulating/handling
	KINESTHETIC (external)	50 experiencing/doing
	Kinesthetic (internal)	50 feeling/intuition
MOBILITY	stationary 50	30 movement needed

Explanation

When students have to learn difficult content their performance will be strongly influenced by their biorhythm – their time-of-day preferences.

School timetables follow a similar pattern worldwide: academic subjects are scheduled mainly in the morning and non-academic subjects in the afternoon. This generally matches teachers' time preferences but is not good for students who seem to have a different biorhythm from adults and can't concentrate well in the morning. The two group profiles opposite show these significant differences and whenever we compare adult with student results, we find a similar situation. This is a huge disadvantage for the majority of high-school students who find it very hard to concentrate during periods in the early morning and generally wake up before lunch. In primary schools it is similar and although there is a lot of experimentation going on, one school found the ideal schedule to restructure their day.

I found this at Forbury Primary School in Dunedin, New Zealand where the new schedule has made a huge positive impact, and their timetable now looks like this:

Session 1: 9.00-10.00am (10 minutes break)

Session 2: 10.10-11.10am (10 minutes break)

Session 3: 11.20-12.20pm (45 minutes lunch break)

Session 4: 1.05-2.05pm (10 minutes break)

Session 5: 2.15-3.00pm (end of school day)

During Session 1 difficult curriculum content is generally not taught – the hour is used for revision, non-academic subjects and even sports. As that might not be possible at other schools, teachers need to match most other students' learning needs when difficult content has to be taught during times which are students' non-preferences. Teachers can also compensate by adding multisensory activities, background music and energizing exercises.

Information

Need for intake and mouth stimulation

Explanation

Research has shown that analytic, more left-brain dominant students find eating, nibbling, chewing and drinking quite distracting and do not need mouth stimulation while they learn.

However, holistic, right-brain dominant students need mouth stimulation to enhance their concentration. They will chew anything they can get hold of – pens, pencils, paper, hair, clothes or fingernails, particularly when they are impatient, bored, stressed or frustrated.

Even if eating in class or chewing gum is not allowed in school, students with a strong need for intake will find something to chew on. Instead of telling them off, teachers need to discuss this biological need with their students and find strategies that allow them to satisfy their need without making a mess or disrupting learning. For this reason only water in bottles and healthy snacks should be allowed and all sweet drinks and sugary, sticky snacks have no place in a good learning environment.

TIP:
Snacks are not for everyone; they are only allowed for those students whose LSA profiles show a need for 'Intake', if there is no disruption and their academic performance improves. Students with flexibilities can wait until the break, but there should always be water available.

TIP:
A combined biological need for intake and tactile stimulation is often an indicator that these students are in danger of becoming smokers because cigarettes satisfy the need for finger and mouth stimulation despite the obvious health risk.

Information

Need for sound while learning

Background music needs to be instrumental only – no radio station or pop music. To stimulate brain activity during learning processes, music needs to be selected by its tempo: slower baroque music and more lively classical music show the best results and these four composers below are always safe to choose for enhancing learning.

BAROQUE & CLASSICAL MUSIC

SLOWER:	**MORE LIVELY:**
storing info.	creative activities
text reading	essay writing
reflecting	mind mapping
revision	brain storming
Largo & Adagio Andante	*Classical & Romantic music*
PACHELBEL **ALBINONI**	**VIVALDI** **MOZART**

Explanation

Holistic, right-brain dominant students need sound stimulation to learn better and enhance their concentration whereas analytic, more left-brain dominant students find noises and background music distracting and learn best when it's quiet.

As there are generally more holistic students in primary and secondary schools, which can be a dilemma for those teachers who prefer a quiet classroom. It is true that many students can learn quietly because they are flexible enough to do so, but those who have a strong preference for sound stimulation will not be able to suppress this need and adjust to a quiet classroom. They will make their own sounds and noises when forced to learn in silence and often disrupt quiet work periods because anything for them is better than being quiet.

A good indicator is that noisy students need sound. Chatting and making noises is often the simplest way to have sound stimulation when there is no background music to stimulate their brains. Therefore it is vital for teachers to learn about the use of music in learning.

The most important rules are that music in class has to be enjoyable, is not there for entertainment but solely to enhance students' concentration and learning capacities. Also the use of music for some students should never disrupt the learning of those who need quiet; therefore teachers need to know their students' LS and how to subgroup them according to their needs.

> **TIP:**
> If possible, place students who need sound and music into one area of the classroom, away from those who need quiet.

Information

Creating LS classrooms

These pictures show formal and informal areas in junior and senior classrooms at Forbury Primary School, Dunedin, New Zealand, which accommodate the different style needs of students. All classrooms have varying colour schemes with brighter colours for younger students and more subdued colours for older, more restless students. Coloured fabric is also used to diffuse harsh fluorescent light.

Despite the hi-tech equipment in today's classrooms, they often still resemble traditional, formal settings from the past. They are totally unsuitable for many students who need a very different, more comfortable learning environment. Furniture, colour and lighting play an important role in academic achievement, often overlooked as one of the reasons for learning difficulties.

Information

Why would we want to create classrooms that look more like living rooms when we have so many schools with new furniture and IT equipment? Sadly though, despite hi-tech, refurbished classrooms and modern schools, academic results and achievement levels are going down in many countries. However, around the world I have seen many classrooms based on LS principles bringing about incredibly positive changes.

The sole reason for creating LS classrooms is to achieve higher learning motivation among students, better academic performance and improved classroom discipline. Traditional classrooms with formal arrangement of desks and chairs unfortunately make learning difficult, particularly for underachieving holistic, non-academic students, who usually need comfortable seating, low light, sound and lots of mobility to learn well (see also pages 50-55).

Creating LS classrooms can be a lengthy process, an evolution, starting with small changes, adding further improvements, always involving students and, in primary schools, often their parents, even the wider school community.

When planning to create classrooms that will enhance students' learning by accommodating their true style needs, it is best to make a list of desirable equipment, then secure finances and every possible support, but never forget that all these changes need to be based on students' LSA results and *not* on some personal ideas teachers and students might have for making the learning environment 'nicer' and more 'creative'. Classrooms are functional rooms that should feel good when used and therefore treasured by everyone.

Basic Outfit for Learning Style Classrooms

ICT/AV per classroom:

5 new computers
5 computer consoles
5 swivel chairs
5 Alpha Smart Machines
5 Note Takers
1 tape deck with CD player
1 overhead projector
3 sets of headphones
2 Talking Books
collection of 6 classical music CD's
educational software

for library:

2 new computers
2 computer consoles
2 swivel chairs
10 Talking Books
1 tape deck with CD player
1 TV & video (DVD) machine
3 sets of headphones
collection of 5 classical music CD's
educational software
1 laminating machine (up to A1 size sheets)

Other necessary equipment items per classroom: (3 classrooms, 1 library)

2 couches
2 bean bag chairs
2 inflatable children's seats
1 water dispenser
1 magnetic board
1 display board
1 whiteboard with pens
3 table or clip-on lamps
6 new light tubes (58 Watts, True Light)
2 room dividers
6 low tables
1 trolley for Big Books
2 plastic trays (for creating sand trays)
curtains or blinds
18 filing/.storage boxes (one per student)
3 big cushions
fabrics and paint for making small cushions for each student
collection of Koosh balls (2 Mondo, 5 medium sized, 10 Mini)
3 pot plants
1 set of indoor perceptual motor equipment
1 fan (summer and winter function)
additional power points

This is an example of a 'wish list' for setting up LS classrooms at the beginning of 'Project Forbury' – a successful LS implementation programme, which I instigated and supervised at Forbury Primary School in Dunedin, New Zealand. It was funded by the Ministry of Education and successfully completed over a period of three years

Application

Before beginning to work in newly established LS classrooms, it is most important that the teacher has discussions with students about their personal learning styles, the LSA group profile of the whole class, their new learning environment, how they are going to use it to everyone's benefit and how they will keep it in good shape and functional for the future.

Here are the basic rules for LS classrooms:

- Look at your students' LSA group profiles so that you know who needs informal work areas.

- Share the results with parents, explain what you intend to do and why, then ask for donations of soft furniture and other equipment.

- Make it clear to students that all schoolwork must be completed but can be done anywhere in the classroom as long as discipline is maintained and the teacher can observe everyone.

- Academic achievement of students permitted to work informally must be better or at least as good as before the change to an LS classroom.

- Students who misuse the privilege of using soft furniture will forfeit their right.

- No student's LS need should interfere with or distract anyone with different style preferences.

LS classrooms are easier to establish in primary schools but even in high schools, where classrooms are used by various student groups, it is possible to set up a learning styles environment because the basic components are the same. In very traditional schools these changes will be profound and have to be introduced step-by-step. If done carefully, the results will be positive to a degree hardly imaginable, particularly among students who are known as underachievers and troublemakers.

Rearranging traditional classrooms

Utilizing a crowded space differently in a formal classroom to allow different social groupings and a little privacy

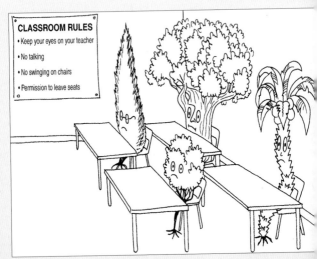

CLASSROOM RULES
- Keep your eyes on your teacher
- No talking
- No swinging on chairs
- Permission to leave seats

Things that don't move don't need a brain

Application

Once students' learning styles are assessed and their results have been discussed, it is time to consider rearranging the current classroom. It might seem that this is a time-consuming process, taking away precious time from teaching the curriculum. Please be assured, it is *not* a waste of time because when students can work in an environment they have helped rearrange, they like the result of their involvement and will learn better, feel better and co-operate with the teacher differently.

First let students draw a plan of their classroom with its current furniture. (This can be a valuable exercise on the computer.) Then discuss with them how it could be transformed into an LS classroom accommodating different style needs to the greatest possible extent. You will be surprised how well your students know what they want and need to enable them to learn well.

Let them come up with ideas about how to get donations from parents and/or the community to furnish their new classroom with more comfortable seating and what needs to be done to lower light levels in the informal areas. Try to involve the caretaker and cleaners so that they know why classrooms are being rearranged, will not put the classroom back into the previous formal set-up and will probably help rather than interfere when the actual work begins.

At this point, it would also be good to let students know *your* learning style, and if it is different from the majority of the class, that you respect their true learning needs but also expect them to be tolerant towards others with different preferences. In this process all of you will become more tolerant and flexible.

TIP:
If students can't learn the way you teach, you have to learn to teach the way they *can* learn.

Practical tips for workflow in class

A classroom rearranged to accommodate various learning needs, including formal and informal areas, dividers and free spaces, desks for working alone, in small groups or as a large group on the floor.

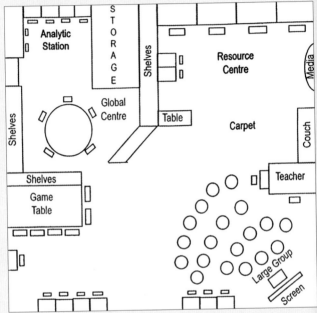

A rearranged classroom such as the one shown above allows for different social groupings, individual work and large group instruction when appropriate. Once students know with whom they work best and which activities they have to do first, they can select where they want to be and have free access to teaching resources. Free movement should be possible for teacher and students. If 'breakout' spaces are available they could be utilized for students who need to work in peace and quiet, which is sometimes difficult in very active classes.

Application

LS classrooms are workrooms where activities follow a certain workflow to achieve the best possible outcome. In every LS classroom students should be able to move between workstations that contain LS tools and are set up to accommodate different activities. Moving from activity to activity also gives students the necessary mobility, if this is their preference. Such a set-up allows learning tasks to be arranged according to students' sensory preferences whereby they start with their strongest sense(s) and then switch to other senses, thus becoming more flexible. In this way, resources can be reused by everyone at different times in the learning process. What might be the first activity for one group of students will come later for others as a reinforcement activity.

It is important for teachers to have a desk, which could be off-limits for students if the teacher chooses and, although it is no longer at the front of the class, the desk should be placed in a strategic spot so that observation of students is possible at all times.

Your teaching will be less stressful when you can plan for a workflow that makes complex tasks easier. The better organized you are with resources and activities, the more relaxed you can be during a lesson and this transmits to your students. Include in your planning not only *what* you are teaching but also *how* and *where from* – you are the stage manager'. The better all your moves are planned, the more you can be free for spontaneity and creativity, yet still following your overall plan. The more preparation – the more freedom!

TIP:

Compare a classroom with your kitchen or workroom at home and transfer the workflow processes to your classroom. It will make your daily work easier and help reduce stress.

Importance of different light levels in classrooms

Group profiles of adults generally show a need for bright light in a large percentage of people in the workplace and among participants in training. They cannot imagine that students could work better under low light. In this group below half the people need bright light and nobody can concentrate well in dim light conditions.

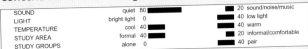

SOUND	quiet	80	20 sound/noise/music
LIGHT	bright light	0	40 low light
TEMPERATURE	cool	40	40 warm
STUDY AREA	formal	40	20 informal/comfortable
STUDY GROUPS	alone	0	40 pair

When interpreting the group profile showing flexibilities, the situation for this group is even more significant. *Everyone* needs bright light – 50 per cent preferences and 50 per cent flexibility – there is nobody who can concentrate well under low light, therefore fluorescent lights will be the right illumination for this group.

SOUND	quiet	40	20 sound/noise/music
LIGHT	bright light	50	50 low light
TEMPERATURE	cool	50	60 warm
WORK AREA	formal	40	40 informal/comfortable
WORKING GROUPS	alone	50	50 pair

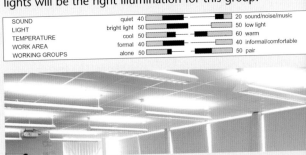

In the group profile below the situation is different: these are teenagers and only 20 per cent prefer bright light and 50 per cent can work under it, but overall 50 per cent can concentrate better under low light conditions. Similar results can be seen in LSA profiles of primary and secondary students – the younger children are, the less light they need, and teachers must accept that.

SOUND	quiet	30	60 sound/noise/music
LIGHT	bright light	50	40 low light
TEMPERATURE	cool	60	40 warm
STUDY AREA	formal	20	40 informal/comfortable
WORKING GROUPS	alone	40	40 pair

Application

most every classroom is equipped with fluorescent lights
at are switched on most of the time. This bright light is
mulating for analytic learners who can concentrate best
artificial light and most teachers need such illumination
well. Unless educators are trained in LS, they hardly
ow about the negative effects of fluorescent light on
dents' brain functions and concentration ability. It
nnot be emphasized often enough that for holistic, right-
ain dominant students these same rays of light cause
peractivity, mental stress, restlessness and a general over-
mulation.

though there is plenty of evidence that low light levels
ve a hugely positive influence on students' behaviour,
found that lowering light levels in classrooms is the
ost difficult LS aspect for teachers because they
emselves need bright light to work. But a solution can be
nd by following these tips:

- Observe who switches on the lights, even on sunny days – it's
  often the teacher and students accept it.

- Consult your students' LSA group results to be sure who needs
  bright or dim light and who is flexible.

- Discuss the need for light with your students. Let them describe
  how it feels having to work under the wrong light level.

- If possible, keep one row of lights on and switch others off. If
  there is only one light switch, remove the fluorescent tubes that
  are not needed but inform the caretaker!

- Turn the lights off in the darkest corner of the classroom and
  permit holistic learners, poor readers and underachievers to sit
  comfortably in these darkened areas. Observe differences in their
  behaviour and attention spans during the first six-week period
  then look for improved achievement. You will be surprised!

Classrooms at St Vincent Primary School in Birmingham h. been set up with comfortable low-light areas and formal are under bright artificial light. Students are allowed to choc their work areas according to their LSA preferences for lig

Application

you have many students who need low light, cover large, right white surfaces in the classroom when they are not in se. Choose subdued colours if your students are restless or iagnosed with ADHD as it will calm them down. In lassrooms with too many windows, create dim light areas y covering certain windows permanently with darker loth, curtains or blinds to block out sunlight. Use coloured heets of fabrics, at a safe distance away from the light ource to diffuse fluorescent light. With such measures you vill also achieve a tent-like effect, make classrooms more olourful and cosy (see the picture on page 62).

his might provoke you, but it is a cheap and effective way f helping students to work under reduced light levels, articularly when the majority of your students need bright ght. Allow those who have shown a preference for low ght in their LSA profile to wear sunglasses or sun-visors vhen they squint, when they ask for that privilege or when hey appear uncomfortable in too much light. What seem o be 'normal' light levels for teachers or other adults are ften too bright for many students.

Vhen you work with underachievers, turn the lights off ntirely. Stretch your own flexibilities and teach in low atural light. Monitor the effects on students' behaviour nd their concentration span in low light.

)iscuss with your students the biological need for different ight levels and inform parents about this important issue o that they can provide the right lighting for their children t home when they do their homework. Siblings often leed different light levels and parents need much more ight than their children. The older we get, the more light ve need!

TIP:
Tell them how much light *you* need and that you are willing to match their need, even if it's too dark for you. They will love you for that!

How colours influence learning

*Soothing colours at the Learning Centre a
Cramlington Community High School, Northumberland, UI
with space for kinesthetic learning in the hallway*

*A once-derelict inner courtyard was transformed into a Zen garden a
Tumbarumba High in a hot area of New South Wales in Australi*

Explanation

Often classrooms are either too cluttered or walls are stark and monotonous. The best would be a comfortable middle ground. In combination with colour, lighting is of utmost importance and natural light and full-spectrum lighting is the best.

Mood can affect behaviour as well as attitude and the colors in a room can directly influence teachers' and students' moods. Specific colours encourage certain emotions and brightly coloured walls are not appropriate for classrooms. Wall colours can be warm or cool tones, but keep the colours fairly light and not greyed.

Deep 'warm' colours give classrooms an intimate, cosy feeling (red-violet, red, red-orange, orange, terracotta, yellow-orange, yellow) and in combination with navy blue can achieve a quietly stimulating effect. These colours are useful in cold climates with long winters.

Light 'cool' colours make a classroom seem more spacious, have a calming effect (green, blue-green, blue-violet; white also have this effect) and are particularly good for schools in temperate climates.

The school environment is also important and can have a very soothing influence on agitated students when designed with human beings in mind. Instead of concrete there should be lots of plants, which help create a relaxed atmosphere like the Zen garden opposite, which has become a favourite spot for students.

You will find more information on colour on the following websites:

www.rockymountainprinting.com and www.glidden.com

Information on lighting can be found at:

www.narva-bel.de and www.naturallighting.com

Full spectrum light is available as BioLight in Europe and is marketed in the USA as Vita-Lite.

Learning Styles at school and at home

Information

Different uses of LS in primary and secondary schools

During the early years of education learning styles change dramatically and teachers need to be familiar with style preferences of students when they enter school and understand how biological style features change and grow until they move on to secondary school.

Parent working bees at Tumbarumba High, Australia sewing curtains to create low light areas in classroom

Style needs in students vary according to their age but they always have them – at home or in class. Teachers and parents need to understand these differences and allow students to learn in their own way, providing support not as they see fit as adults but as it is truly needed by the youngsters.

Explanation

Compared to primary schools the situation in secondary schools is very different and implementation of LS has to be adjusted to accommodate far more impersonal learning environments (albeit often hi-tech), academic expectations, curriculum and exam pressure as well as information overload and stressed-out teachers and students.

Teachers have no time and hardly any means to deliver personalized instructions and therefore LSA-Senior reports are invaluable; they contain a diagnosis of a student's preferred style plus a detailed study guide which puts more responsibility on students to do their schoolwork in a way which is best for them. This however requires that schools provide learning environments suited to students' natural styles, financial means to assess students' LSAs at least twice during high-school years and teachers who are trained in using teaching strategies that match their students' learning needs.

As long as exam results are still acceptable and discipline is manageable, a deeper knowledge of LS is often seen as a luxury the school cannot afford. We often find that schools are prepared to use LSA instruments only when underachievement and academic failure have increased dramatically and attainment has fallen to unacceptable levels. Then they begin with LS applications and teachers are surprised that positive results are achievable within six weeks. Because high-school teachers generally have to deal with large student numbers, LSA group profiles give them detailed information about the learning needs of whole classes so that personalized teaching can be introduced to whole groups and monitored for success.

LSA profiles help students to understand how they learn best, in class and at home, how to use their personal strengths and how to become more flexible.

Information

Personalized teaching in lecture theatres and science labs

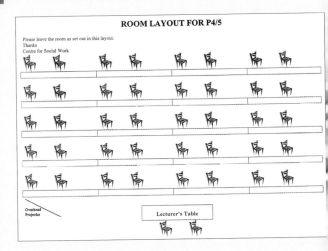

ROOM LAYOUT FOR P4/5

Please leave the room as set out in this layout.
Thanks
Centre for Social Work

Overhead Projector

Lecturer's Table

In traditional classrooms and fixed-furniture laboratories it is more difficult to accommodate LS needs, but it is possible by compensating with multisensory teaching methods, music in the background for holistic students, and allowing some movement and social groupings according to personal learning needs.

FAIR

in this classroom does not mean

that everyone gets the SAME

but that everyone gets what they

NEED

Explanation

When teaching in formal classrooms and lecture theatres, it is more important than anywhere else for students to understand their personal LS and to discuss how their learning needs can be accommodated under such difficult conditions. This will help them become more flexible and learn to compensate when their styles cannot be matched.

In lecture theatres:

- always use multisensory teaching methods;

- use good visuals with big print and colours;

- switch during your presentation from analytic to holistic and practise 'double tracking';

- change light levels if possible to have bright and dim light areas;

- use background music to enhance brain functions of your students;

- initiate short movement breaks;

- allow healthy nibbles and water bottles but no soft drinks (sugar is a learning killer!);

- have 'buzz groups' after lecturing for no longer than 15-20 minutes;

- be interactive and involve students;

- encourage them to study at home through their preferences in an environment conducive to learning.

In labs and fixed-furniture classrooms:

- know your students' learning styles;

- do as many of the above activities appropriate for lecture theatres;

- allow students who need quiet to wear disconnected headsets or earplugs for their work periods;

- ask students how the existing work environment could be utilized more effectively to match styles – you might be surprised about the useful and workable ideas your students have because they know how they want to learn!

Information

Learning styles, testing and exams

What happens in Learning?

INTAKE – Processing – Storage of...

...NEW and/or DIFFICULT information

What happens at Exams?

OUTPUT of information not necessarily through one's personal learning style.

Exams are:
OUTPUT of information

under difficult conditions, often with the brain in reptilian/downshift mode, BUT:

once information is learned/understood through one's personal learning style (= information INTAKE),

confident information OUTPUT happens in many different ways - with success even under exam pressure.

Above are two slides from my Learning Style seminars explaining the profound differences between the processes of information intake and information output to make teachers aware that after studying through LS preferences, good performance in exams is nearly always guaranteed – students want to show what they know

Information

From research on the original LS instruments as well as from anecdotal evidence and practical experience with our LSA instruments we know that test and exam results improve when students have been allowed to learn and prepare themselves in their own best way, based on their personal learning style.

In short: LS teaching improves grades and test results.

Therefore teachers need to be aware that:

■ during the presentation of new and/or difficult curriculum content students' strong LS preferences must be accommodated whenever possible to ensure concentration, motivation and the best learning outcome;

■ when students know their LS and have learned about different study techniques, they will be able to prepare themselves more effectively by using the guidelines from their LSA reports;

■ encouraging students to learn 'their way' in class and at home is the best guarantee of exam success;

■ allow water and healthy snacks during written exams and, ideally, also small things for tactile stimulation for those students who need it;

■ during tests and exams LS applications are not so crucial because most students have enough flexibilities to cope with adverse situations. This is especially true when the learning process preceding the exam has been accomplished with teaching methods matched to their personal LS preferences. Through LS strategies students learn, understand and remember better and are much more confident in showing what they know in exam situations. Even when their personal learning styles are not being matched during the exam, they are less prone to failure or having memory lapses because with LS-based study techniques, curriculum content is more readily available, even under pressure.

Information

LSA: Parent Version

 LSA-Junior: Parent Version

Susie Sample

Profile Summary

Susie's preferences are her strengths when she can use them in difficult learning situations. Her non-preferences become her weaknesses when she has to use them often. This can lead to frustration, concentration problems, low motivation, and learning difficulties. It is best when she is allowed to learn HER way - in school, at home and later in life.

Key elements of Susie's style
when she has to learn something NEW and/or DIFFICULT:

Susie's Preferences: (How she learns best)

BRAIN DOMINANCE: sequential	
SENSORY MODALITIES: auditory (hearing), auditory (external), visual (external), kinesthetic (internal)	
PHYSICAL NEEDS: stationary, no intake, afternoon	
ENVIRONMENT: quiet, warm, formal study area	
SOCIAL: parent authority	
ATTITUDES: self-starting, conforming, other-directed	

Susie's Non-Preferences: (What she needs to avoid when learning something difficult)

BRAIN DOMINANCE:	none
SENSORY MODALITIES: kinesthetic (external)	

ENVIRONMENT

SOUND - quiet: (preference)
Susie really needs it quiet while concentrating, reading or writing. She can learn best when it's silent at home and to improve her concentration, she should work in a quiet study area with carpeted, noise reducing floors. She should also use ear plugs to cut out distracting noises. To do her homework well, she needs a quiet place with very few distractions.

LIGHT - low: (flexibility)
Susie's need for light while doing her homework is dependent on what she does. When she is interested in her learning tasks, light is not really important to her, but generally she prefers not having too much bright light in her study area. Although she doesn't always need low light when she studies, she doesn't really like bright light all the time around her either.

TEMPERATURE - warm: (preference)
Susie prefers to learn where temperatures are warm and comfortable. Therefore she probably learns better during the warmer months of the year. As she finds it difficult to concentrate when it is too cold for her, ensure that she is allowed to use additional heaters or wear extra clothing to keep warm.

STUDY AREA - formal: (preference)
Susie studies best in a more formal environment, and tends to read or do her homework better sitting upright in a chair at a desk or table. Whenever she needs to concentrate, make sure that she is not sitting on soft furniture or stretched out - she might fall asleep! A formal, office-like set-up or work area at home is more effective for her.

Extracts from the Parent Version of a student's LSA profile
and report, giving detailed descriptions of a child's best
ways of learning new and/or difficult information at home

Explanation

The parent versions of the LSA-Junior and LSA-Senior profiles have been created to allow parents a better insight into their children's LS. Research has shown that parents often have a very different LS from their children and won't accept that they can learn well with so called 'distractions' like background music, sprawling out on a bed or the floor, nibbling, or moving around. Whether they like it or not, this is exactly how many teenagers (who are holistic, right-brain dominant) can learn best.

When interpreting LSA profiles parents need to:

- find strong preferences and look at the combination of needs – different combinations result in very different academic performance and behaviour;

- look out for non-preferences and see how they clash with their own LS, beliefs about 'good' learning and how their children should do homework;

- specifically look at preferences and flexibilities in the sensory modalities. The more strong preferences a child has, the easier information intake is, and the more flexibilities a child has, the more their learning success will depend on interest in the topic and motivation to learn;

- discuss LSA results with their children, ideally have their own LSA-Adult profile to compare style differences and/or similarities, accept that their children might learn best in a different way from their parents;

- help setting up the best possible physical learning environment at home which cannot always be shared with siblings due to style differences;

- check the question marks in their child's LSA profile – the more there are, the more stress the child is currently experiencing. This is a warning sign – an indication that their child is under pressure and might need help!

What *not* to do with learning styles

DON'T assume all students can learn the same way you do
What makes sense for you in learning (like step-by-step approaches) might be very confusing for students who have a different thinking style.

DON'T label students according to their preferences in sensory modalities
There are no so-called 'visual' or 'kinesthetic' students because they all have combinations of at least two sensory preferences (some have six and more!).

DON'T focus on non-preferences of students
Accept them and focus on preferences and flexibilities – every student has personal strengths in their profile.

DON'T give up on underachievers
They can become very successful learners once their non-traditional learning style combination is understood and matched accordingly in teaching.

DON'T forget that each learning style classroom must have a comfortable area
Those students who need it can learn informally on soft furniture or on the floor.

DON'T ever remove all desks from a classroom
There will always be some students who need to sit uprigh at a desk and those who prefer informal seating need to become more flexible.

DON'T expect that all students in your class have the same or similar learning styles
Consult the LSA group profile to see the style differences (but also similarities) that will guide you in subgrouping your students.

Application

What to *do* when using **LS** in class

Explain to students that the LSA is not a test; that nobody can pass or fail. Inform parents that there is no such thing as a correct or better LS profile.

Accept that each LS classroom must have a comfortable area with dim lighting where students can learn informally on soft furniture or on the floor. This is even possible in high schools!

Avoid switching on the lights in a classroom because *you* need them. Younger students need much less light than adults and get agitated under fluorescent lights.

Involve pupils in creating the best possible learning environment, let them help design a classroom where everyone can learn really well, and use group profile results as the basis for rearranging classrooms.

Subgroup students according to their sensory preferences and match their other learning needs when teaching new and/or difficult content.

Switch between holistic and analytic approaches, give an overview first, then the necessary details.

Use multisensory teaching strategies, LS tools, music in the background and allow snacks and movement for those who need it.

Remove privileges like soft furniture or snacks when discipline deteriorates and students take advantage. Reintroduce them when discipline and academic achievements improve.

Find out your own teaching style – it will help you become more flexible and accommodate students' learning needs much better.

Information

Teaching Style Analysis (TSA-Ed)

Teaching Style Analysis™

The TSA-Ed pyramid model contains similar elements to the LSA pyramid except that social aspects have been integrated into another layer and a different layer has been added: Lesson/ Unit Planning, which assesses the teaching techniques educators

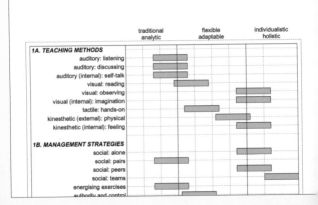

Graph 1: Teaching Style

	traditional analytic	flexible adaptable	individualistic holistic
1A. TEACHING METHODS			
auditory: listening			
auditory: discussing			
auditory (internal): self-talk			
visual: reading			
visual: observing			
visual (internal): imagination			
tactile: hands-on			
kinesthetic (external): physical			
kinesthetic (internal): feeling			
1B. MANAGEMENT STRATEGIES			
social: alone			
social: pairs			
social: peers			
social: teams			
energising exercises			
authority and control			

Without knowing one's own teaching style it is much more difficult for teachers to reach students who have a very different learning style. Although personalized teaching initially requires more effort, the outcomes are profound and have transformed whole schools, even communities. In addition, this self-knowledge helps reduce stress in daily classroom teaching.

Explanation

The TSA-Ed is a professional self-development tool for practising educators. Like the LSA, it is based on a pyramid model and consists of graphs, detailed personal reports and an action plan.

For each graph there is an in-depth description of the teacher's general and personal results, and an action plan can be completed for each sector wherever changes are desired. The monitoring system at the end provides valuable help for implementing the selected new strategies on a daily basis, through which personal progress can be monitored and techniques adjusted.

 TSA-Education Elizabeth Sample

PERSONAL REPORT AND PROFESSIONAL DEVELOPMENT GUIDELINES

GRAPH 1: Your Teaching Style - Overall Scores

-50 to -20
If your score for any of the elements is between -50 and -20 your teaching style in that particular area is considered traditional or highly analytic.
When most of your scores fall within this area, it is a warning signal that you are still using a formal, out-dated way of teaching which might not suit the majority of your students. For becoming more aware of your students' true learning needs you should have their learning styles assessed. By understanding your students' LSA profiles and adopting new teaching methods you will be able to match your teaching style to their individual styles of information intake. When you plan and execute a teaching session, simply remember human diversity. You can then probably move into the next score group - flexible/adaptable.

-20 to +20
If your score for any of the elements is between -20 and +20, your teaching style in that particular area is considered flexible or in transition from traditional, formal teaching to more individualised, holistic instruction methods and you are probably also very adaptable to your students' learning needs. If most of your scores fall within this area, this must be an exciting time for you, full of experiments, creativity, learning and exploring. Good luck with your personal and professional growth, you are on the right track!

+20 to +50
If your score for any of the elements is between +20 and +50, your teaching style in that particular area is considered learner-centred or holistic. If most of your scores fall within this area, you have already embraced the new way of teaching based on human diversity and creativity. Congratulations and keep up the good work!

1A. TEACHING METHODS (Multi-Sensory)

This graph describes your sensory teaching methods which are often based on your personal learning style. The results refer to the way you transfer knowledge to your students by stimulating their senses.

YOUR PERSONAL SCORE

Your current teaching methods seem to be spread from traditional/analytic to flexible/adaptable and individualistic/holistic approaches in the sensory areas. Please keep using the methods which already cater for individual learning needs. Your flexibility allows you to adjust to different learning styles your students will display when using their senses during the learning process. However, in certain areas you still tend to use traditional, analytic methods for all students. Please note that these methods might be suitable for only some of your students but often not for the majority. A valuable help in determining which sensory teaching methods would suit your students' learning needs best is by finding out their individual learning styles and then altering your traditional teaching strategies accordingly.

Information

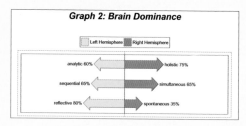

Graph 2: Brain Dominance

Left Hemisphere | Right Hemisphere

analytic 60% ⟷ holistic 75%

sequential 65% ⟷ simultaneous 65%

reflective 80% ⟷ spontaneous 35%

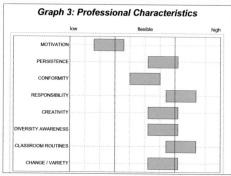

Graph 3: Professional Characteristics

low | flexible | high

MOTIVATION

PERSISTENCE

CONFORMITY

RESPONSIBILITY

CREATIVITY

DIVERSITY AWARENESS

CLASSROOM ROUTINES

CHANGE / VARIETY

TSA-Education

Elizabeth Sample

A few questions worth considering:
Is your preparation mostly concerned with teaching curriculum content or do you use methods for teaching to individual students, allowing the learning process to flow?
Are you using diagnostic tools (like LSA™) to assess your students' learning styles?
Do you create/include self-correcting learning tools for all your students?
Do you orchestrate social interactions during your teaching sessions in class?
Do you pre-plan how and with whom your students will do certain exercises and learning activities?
Does your planning include tasks for individual students, small groups and/or the whole class?
Are you providing a set structure for your students or do you allow them to self-structure their learning tasks?

MY SELF-ENHANCEMENT ACTION PLAN 1D:

1. **WHAT** can I do to make my Planning Techniques more effective for students? (my **GOAL**)
2. **HOW** will I do this? (my **ACTION**)
3. **WHEN** will I take concrete action to achieve the desired outcomes with my new planning techniques? (my **TIME FRAME**)

IN GENERAL:
1. WHAT? ....

2. HOW? ....

3. WHEN? ....

IN A SPECIFIC SUBJECT AREA:
1. WHAT? ....

2. HOW? ....

3. WHEN? ....

GRAPH 2: Brain Dominance

The categories in this graph are arranged in three groups:
A high score in any of these elements indicates a preference for a particular style of thinking, processing thoughts and approaching your work in class.

Similar scores within any of the groups (e.g., 60% for analytic, 66% for holistic) indicate that you are able to switch between the two modes.

High scores in both left and right hemispheres (80% and above) indicate that you are highly integrated in your mental techniques, utilising both brain hemispheres equally strongly.

YOUR PERSONAL SCORE

Explanation

A person's LS greatly influences their teaching style. Through using the TSA a teacher can find out if their style matches the learning needs of their students. These insights, plus the action plan built into the instrument, can be used to develop flexibilities and new teaching strategies to reach particularly those students who have a very different learning style.

When using one of the Self-Enhancement Action Plans (see the example below) we advise teachers only to choose one area at a time because otherwise change can become overwhelmingly complex.

For more information visit:
www.creativelearningcentre.com/default.asp?page=lsat

 TSA-Education   Elizabeth Sample

YOUR PERSONAL SCORE

Presently several of your **Professional Characteristics** seem to be already high in certain areas and your flexibility in others enables you to change and/or improve your attitudes according to the situation or if it makes sense to you. Keep using your flexibility to increase your positive attitudes so that ultimately you will have them all in the high area. This usually leads to increased job satisfaction, creative energy and better cooperation with students, colleagues and superiors. Use your Personal Action Plan for achieving such goals.

MY SELF-ENHANCEMENT ACTION PLAN 3:

1. **WHICH** element(s) in my Professional Characteristics cause stress, frustration, dissatisfaction and burnout in my daily work? (my **REASON**)
2. **WHAT** can I do to become more positive? (my **GOAL**)
3. **HOW** will I do this? (my **ACTION**)
4. **WHEN** will I take concrete action to experience/build a more satisfying set of attitudes to lower my stress levels? (my **TIME FRAME**)

IN CLASS:
1. WHICH?
2. WHAT?
3. HOW?
4. WHEN?

AT MY SCHOOL:
1. WHICH?
2. WHAT?
3. HOW?
4. WHEN?

At the end of each TSA profile there is a Personal Monitoring System through which each Action Plan can be implemented in a way so that the desired changes can actually begin to happen

Natural matches of teaching and learning styles

Finnish Brain Gym® poster and informal classroom in a learning centr in Helsinki. Here teachers and students work in harmon

Tules Mukaan, Finlands Fysioterapeutvörbund 200•

Explanation

Every teacher and student has memories of learning situations that felt good, were enjoyable and had a successful outcome. This happens when teaching and learning styles match naturally, when the student receives curriculum content in a way that matches their preferences and the teacher naturally uses a matching style. The accompanying feeling is that student and teacher are on 'the same wavelength', a state that is always positive and enjoyable.

This however does not happen in schools often enough. Frequently teachers have to stretch their teaching skills to the limit to get some learning out of their students, who also have to stretch their own abilities to suit the way the teacher wants them to participate. More often than not, neither style is met. The result is that schoolwork is more difficult for everyone involved.

But it doesn't have to be like that. If teachers are willing to teach to their students' LS preferences and are trained in LS applications, matches can be created for whole classes and learning success and satisfaction significantly improved.

Once the teacher has accepted the style diversity among their students, other important prerequisites for matching teaching and learning are LSA group profiles, LS classrooms with informal, comfortable areas (as in the picture opposite) and learning tools.

To keep students in the best possible mental state for learning and allow them the necessary mobility, it is most advisable to do regular Brain Gym® activities (also called callisthenics or crossover exercises). The poster opposite was part of a recent campaign in Finnish schools to promote such exercises.

Information

How to start LS programmes in schools

A 12-step quick guide

1. Start with one day of in-service LS training.

2. Assess students' learning styles with the LSA instrument.

3. Interpret LSA results with a trained facilitator.

4. Carry out an observation period of at least seven school days.

5. Share LSA results with students, organize a parent evening.

6. Introduce multisensory teaching methods. Subgroup students according to their preferences.

7. Adapt teaching strategies to suit analytic and holistic students.

8. Begin with classroom redesign based on group profiles. Involve students.

9. Introduce LS tools and let students create their own tools.

10. Monitor and evaluate the change process carefully.

11. Incorporate new students and teachers into the school's new LS approaches.

12. Become a model school, demonstrating LS to others.

Explanation

Monitoring and evaluating the change process

The strategies below have been successfully applied by individual teachers and whole schools in different countries and are recommended as guidelines.

1. Use existing academic records or asses students' academic work (in maths, English, reading and so on) *before* the planned LS programme is introduced. Assess students' learning styles, then follow through with the LS programme for at least three months. After that period assess students again in the same subject areas. Continue with the LS application for another three to six months and then conduct a final assessment of students' achievement in the same subject areas. Academic results from before and after the LS intervention can thus be documented statistically.

2. Establish a trial and a control group, eliciting from both groups students' attitudes, behaviour, learning motivation, overall discipline and any other issues important to class/school development. Assess the learning styles of the trial group, then use LS intervention in this group but teach the control group as usual for three months. Document all changes in the trial group. Reassess students' attitudes, learning motivation, and so on and compare the results of both groups.

3. Select a group of underachieving students and collect their past poor results in different academic subjects. Assess their learning styles with the LSA and their teachers' teaching styles with the TSA instrument, looking for natural matches. Teach all selected students with matched instructions for at least three months (or better still for a whole school year). Assess their academic achievements as usual at the end of a term or school year, document changes and compare results.

Everyone will be surprised about the improvements!

TIP:
Cutting corners does not pay. LS implementation is an evolutionary process, takes several years and is probably never complete.

Summary

How to personalize teaching

The following statements are from my coaching training and can be used as a credo for a teacher's daily work.

I am your teacher and I will:

- Support you
- Encourage you
- Challenge you
- Listen to you
- Be honest with you
- Respect you
- Learn from you
- Provide you with the most effective teaching methods I know

But I will not do everything for you.

Our classroom is:

- **A Fun place**
- **Safe and positive**
- **A Supportive place**
- **Active and interactive**
- **An environment where you can always ask questions**

Explanation

Final tips for success

Student motivation

Teachers should use LSA instruments to check whether their students are externally or internally motivated. If they are not externally motivated, no amount of reward or withholding privileges is going to change their performance, because they simply won't care, and little rewards are often seen as childish and off-putting.

For externally motivated children, the traditional carrot-or-stick works well, but for those who are internally motivated and still don't participate, individualized approaches might be the solution. It is most likely the case that they *want* to learn, but not in a way the teacher requires, or they are not interested in (for them) boring curriculum content. Internal motivation is the most powerful kind of motivation, provided it is properly channelled.

Need for structure and variety

Check your students' needs for structure/guidance and variety and make sure you match those needs as much as possible in class. If they prefer to self-structure and don't want your close supervision, allow them to decide for themselves how to approach a task.

A reminder

There is no 'good' or 'bad' learning style, just the 'right' way for each student (or groups of students). You have your own learning style, which transmits into your teaching style but will not suit every student. Be more flexible, it can save you a lot of stress!

And finally...

Enjoy the style diversity in your class. Never stop learning new ways to reach every student because they all want to learn – but in their own way!

Further reading

Angelo, Simon (2004) *Study Success: How students get top results in school,* Accelerated Learning Institute, Auckland

Claxton, Guy (2002) *Building Learning Power,* Network Educational Press, Stafford

Dunn, Rita and Griggs, Shirley (2003) *Synthesis of the Dunn and Dunn Learning-Style Model Research: Who, What, When, Where, and So What?,* St. John's University, Jamaica, NY

Hughes, Mike (1999) *Closing the Learning Gap,* Network Educational Press, Stafford

Jensen, Eric (1998) *Teaching With the Brain in Mind,* Association for Supervision and Curriculum Development

Kirk, S., Gallagher, J. and Anastasiow, N. (2003) *Educating Exceptional Children,* Houghton Mifflin Co., Boston

Lucas, B., Greany, T., Rodd, J. and Wicks, R. (2002) *Teaching Pupils how to Learn.* Network Educational Press, Stafford

Mandel, Harvey P. and Marcus, Sander I. (1997) *Could Do Better: Why Children Underachieve and What to Do About It,* Wiley

Prashnig, Barbara (2004) *The Power of Diversity,* Network Educational Press, Stafford

Prashnig, Barbara (2006) *Learning Styles in Action,* Network Educational Press, Stafford

Rimm, Sylvia (2004) *Why Bright Kids Get Poor Grades: And What You Can Do About It,* Random House, New York

Schargel, Franklin P. (2003) *Dropout Prevention Tools,* Eye on Education, Larchmont

Spevak, Peter A. and Karinch, Maryann (2004) E*mpowering Underachievers: How to guide failing kids (8–18) to personal excellence,* New Horizon Press, Fall Hills, NJ

Whitley, Michael D. (2001) *Bright Minds, Poor Grades: Understanding and Motivating your Underachieving Child,* Perigee Trade, New York

Acknowledgements

I never intended to write another book so soon after th publication of my previous one and it would not have bee written were it not for the wonderful editing team at Networ Continuum who encouraged and supported me as always. heartfelt thank you for your professional advice. My gratitud also goes to those who in their daily classroom work have th courage to use learning style concepts and are living proof tha this movement is gaining momentum. It is impossible to nam all the pioneering educators in the many different countries wh have contributed over the years with their reports and feedbac to my previous books and ultimately to this guide book. Thar you to you all and keep up the good work!